SRA

Reading Mastery

Plus

Language Workbook

Level 1

SRA

A Division of The McGraw-Hill Companies

Columbus, Ohio

www.sra4kids.com

SRA/McGraw-Hill

A Division of The McGraw-Hill Companies

Copyright © 2002 by SRA/McGraw-Hill.

Send all inquiries to:
SRA/McGraw-Hill
8787 Orion Place
Columbus, OH 43240-4027

Printed in the United States of America.

ISBN 0-07-569016-0

5 6 7 8 9 POH 06 05

Name

1

Name _____

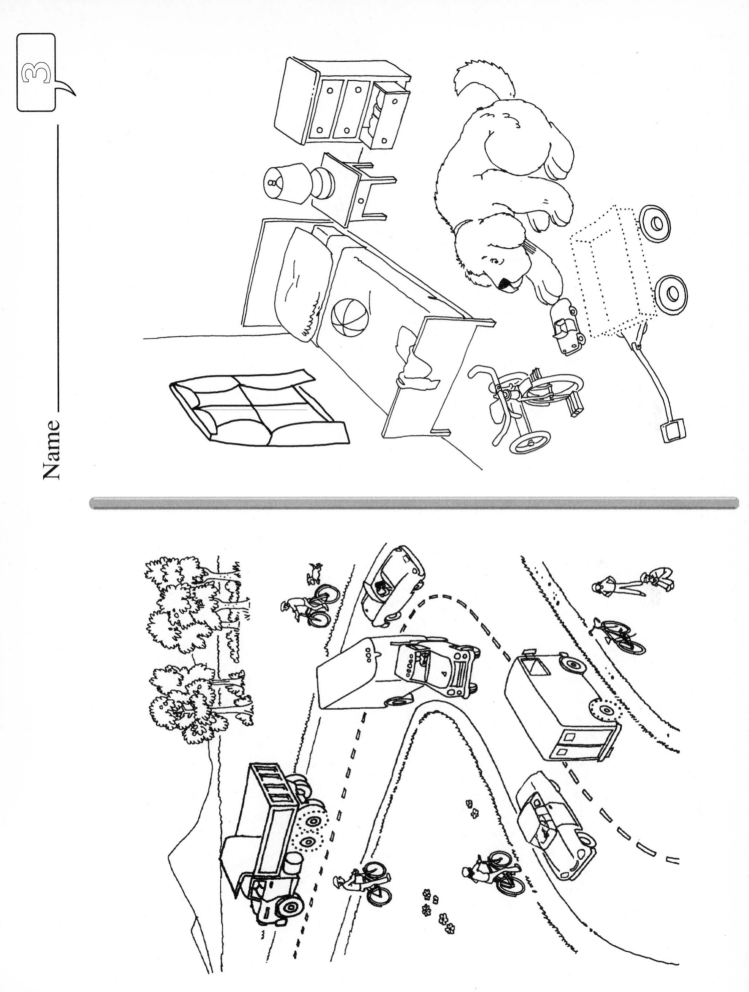

Name

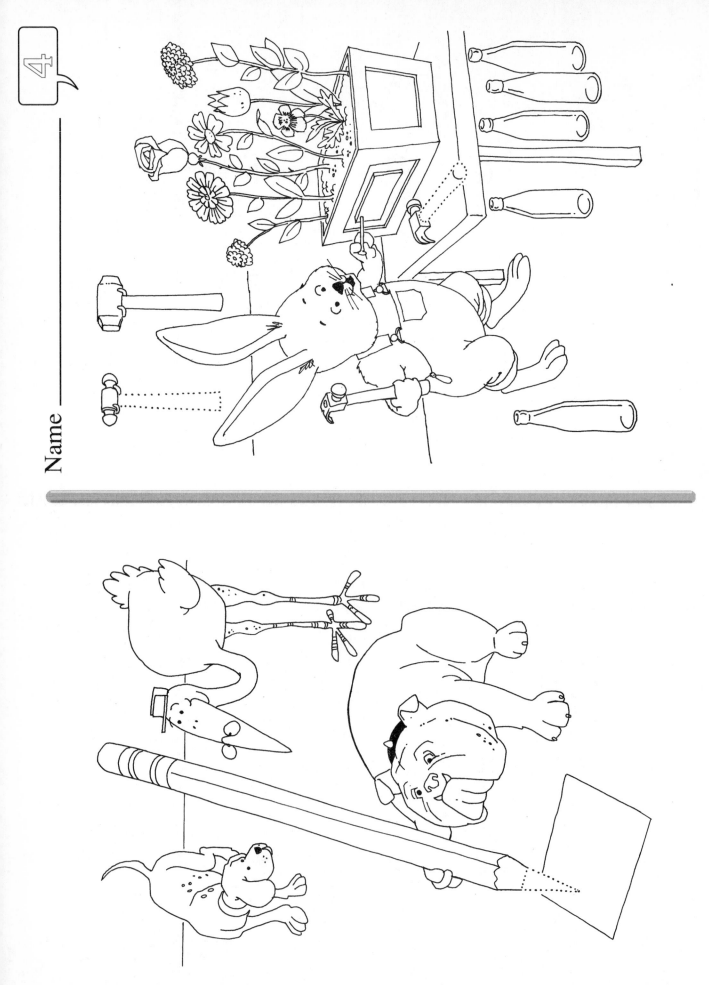

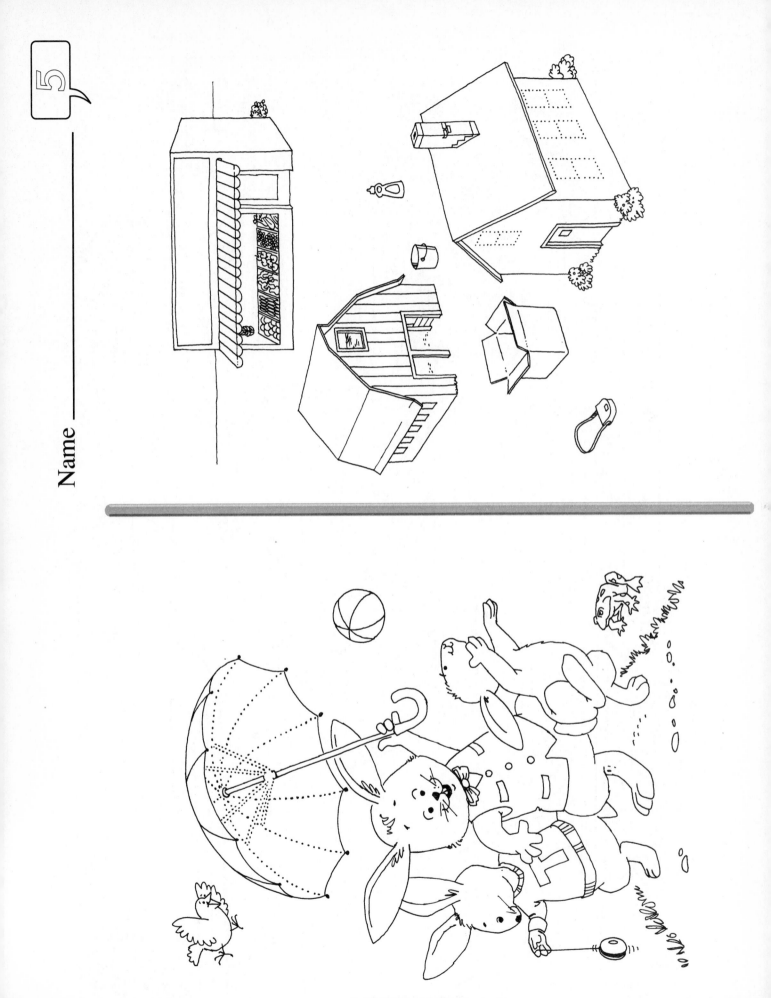

5

Name

Name _____

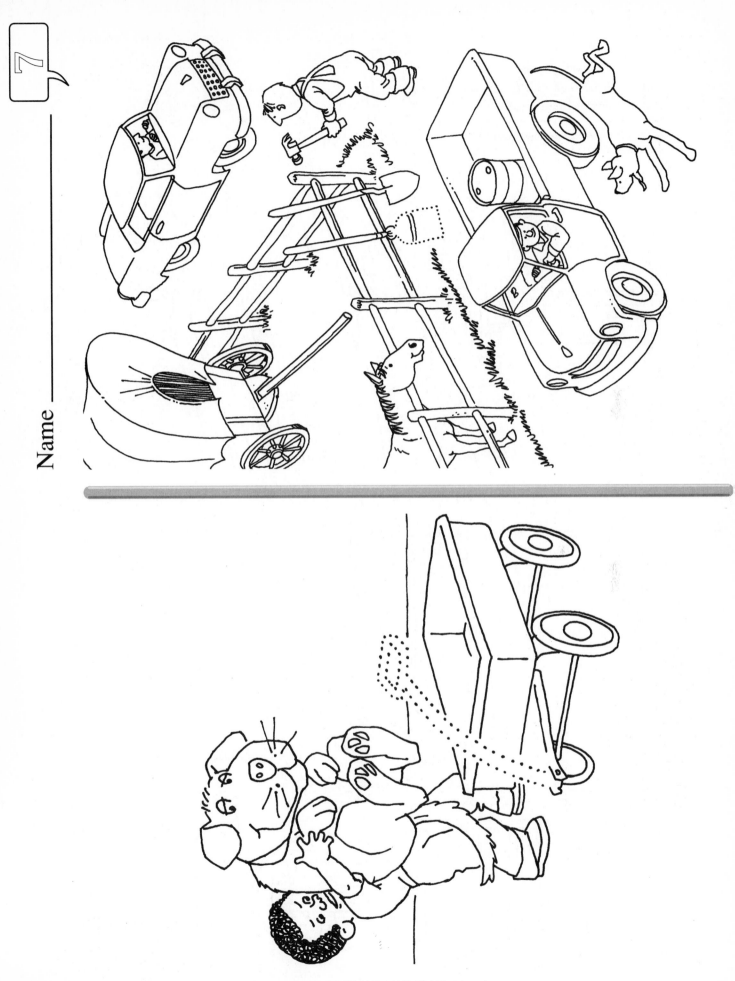

Name

Name

9

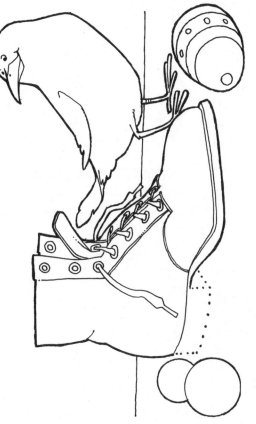

Name

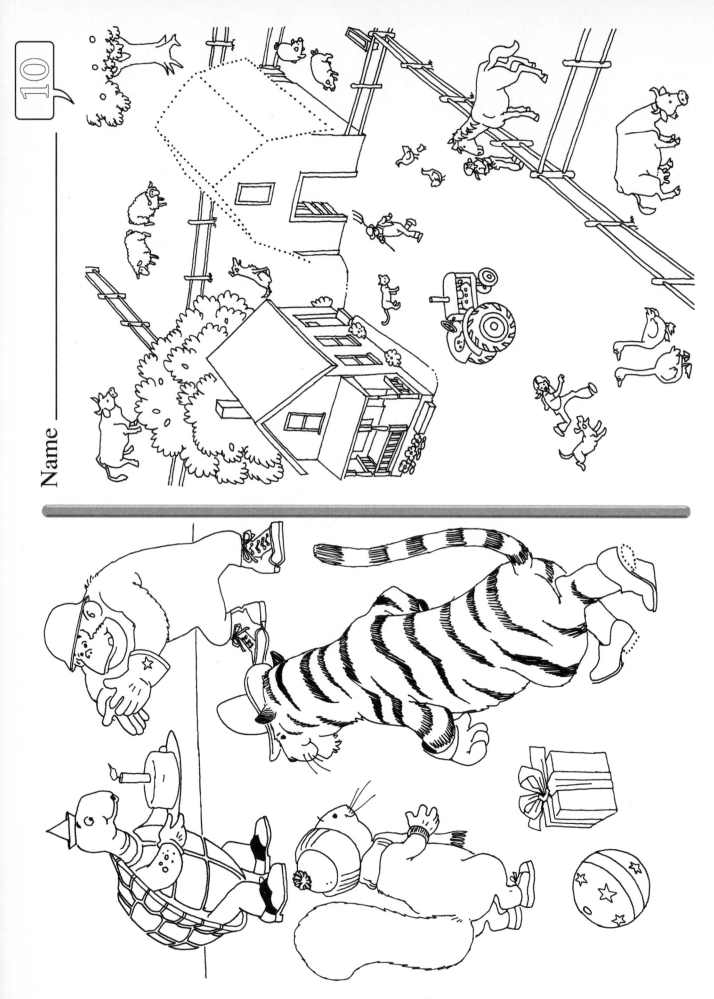

Name

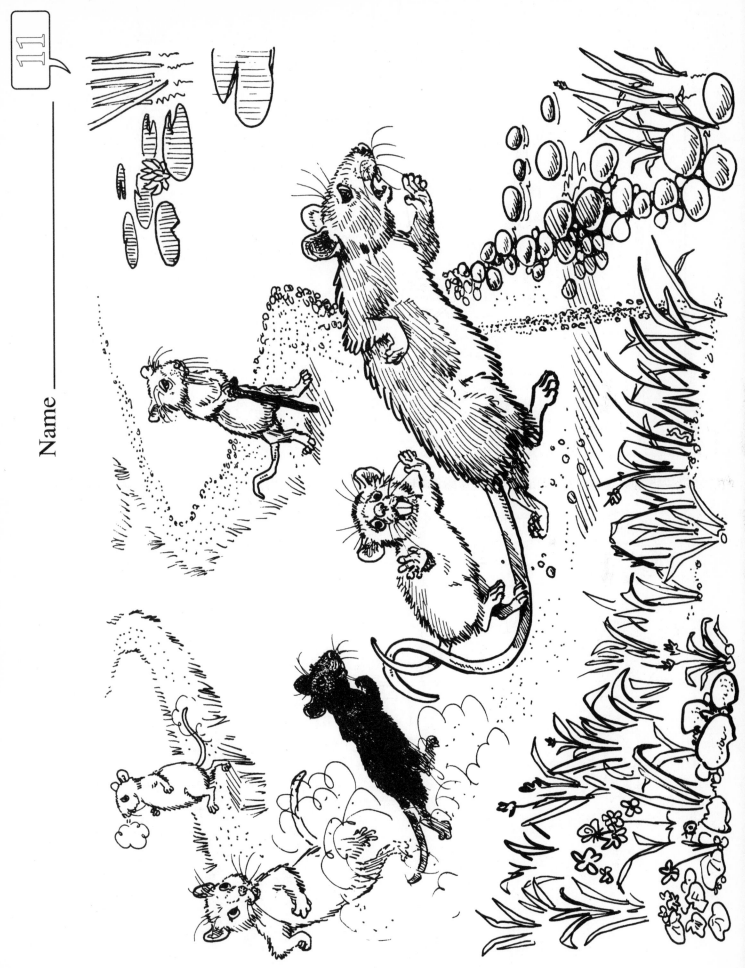

Name _____

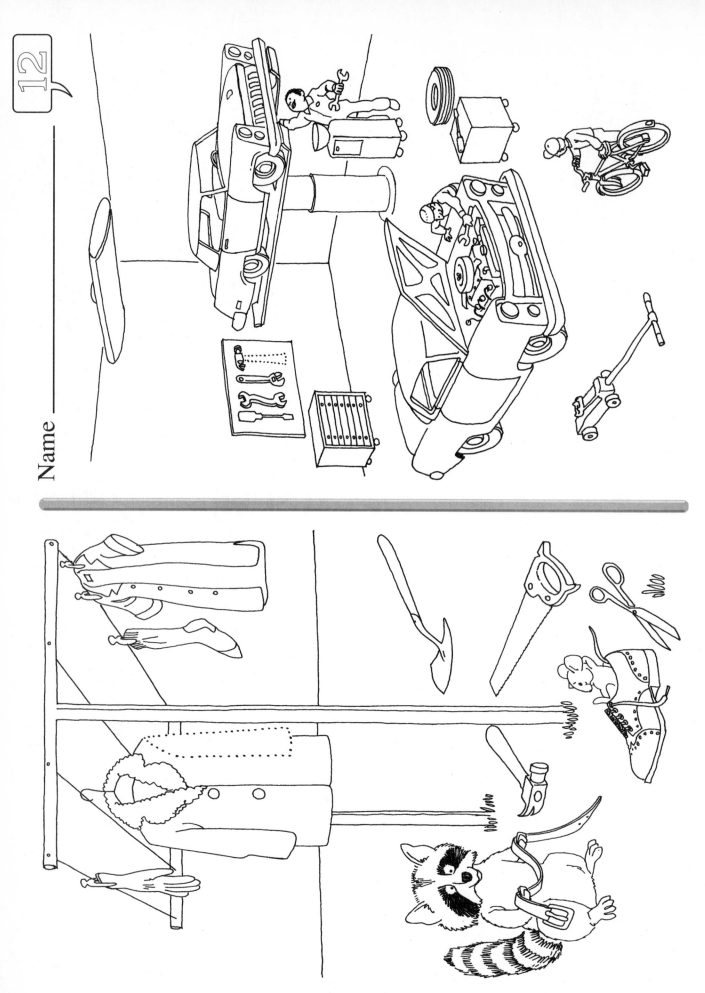

Name _____

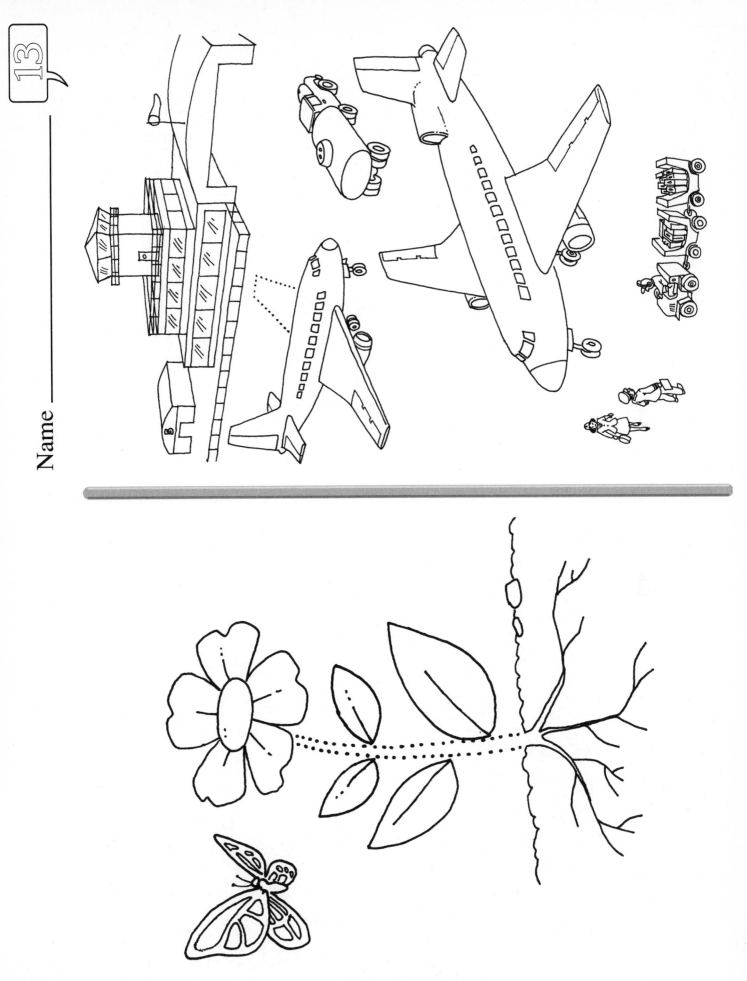

14

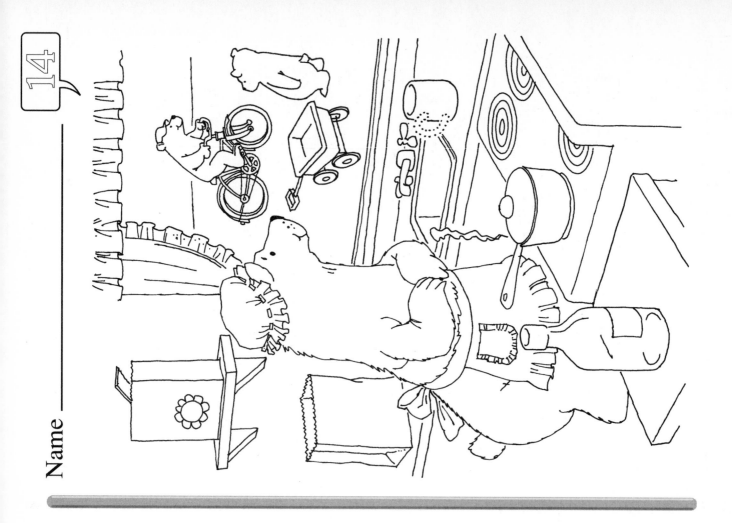

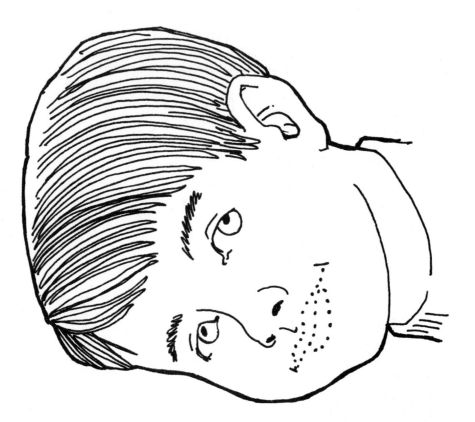

Name _____

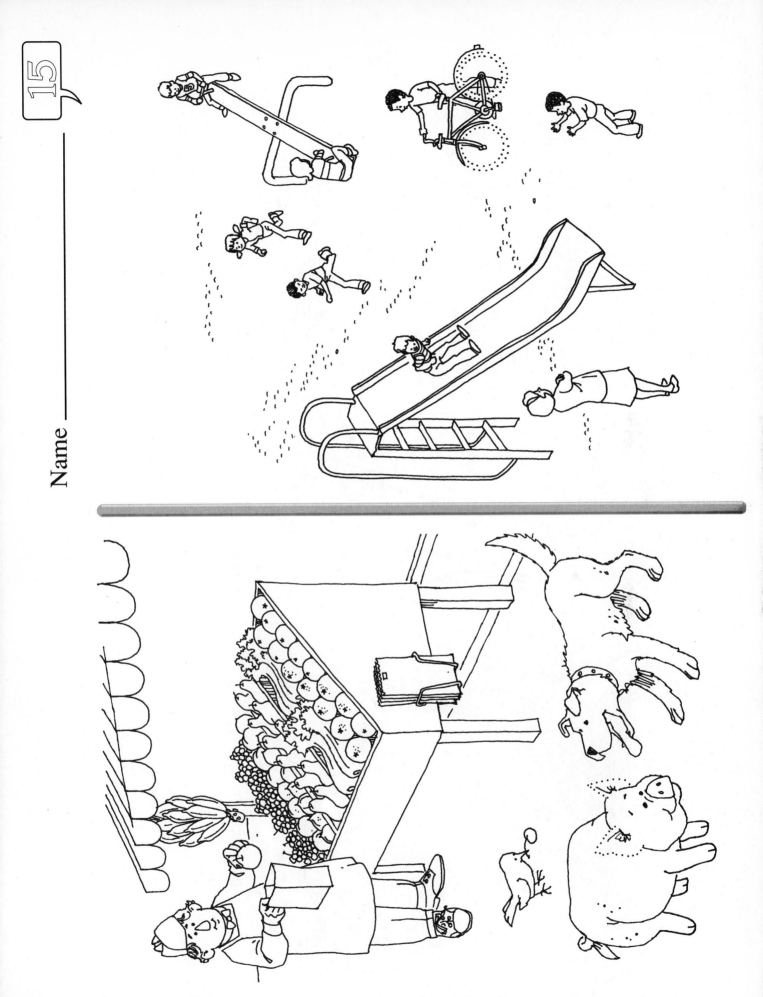

Name

Name _____

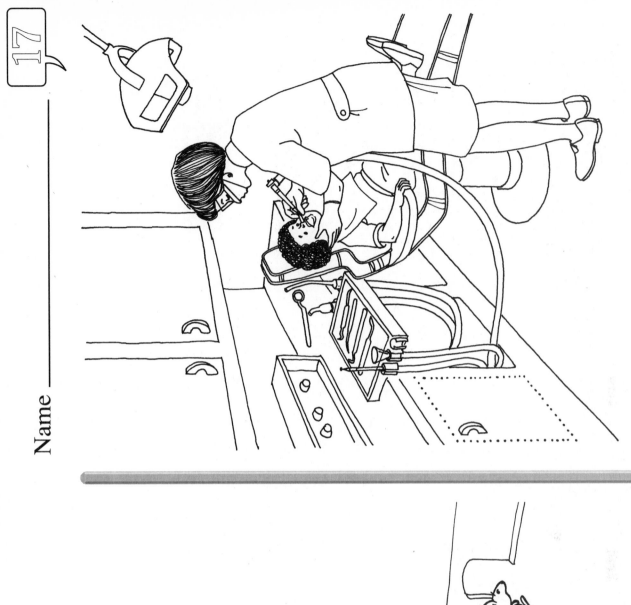

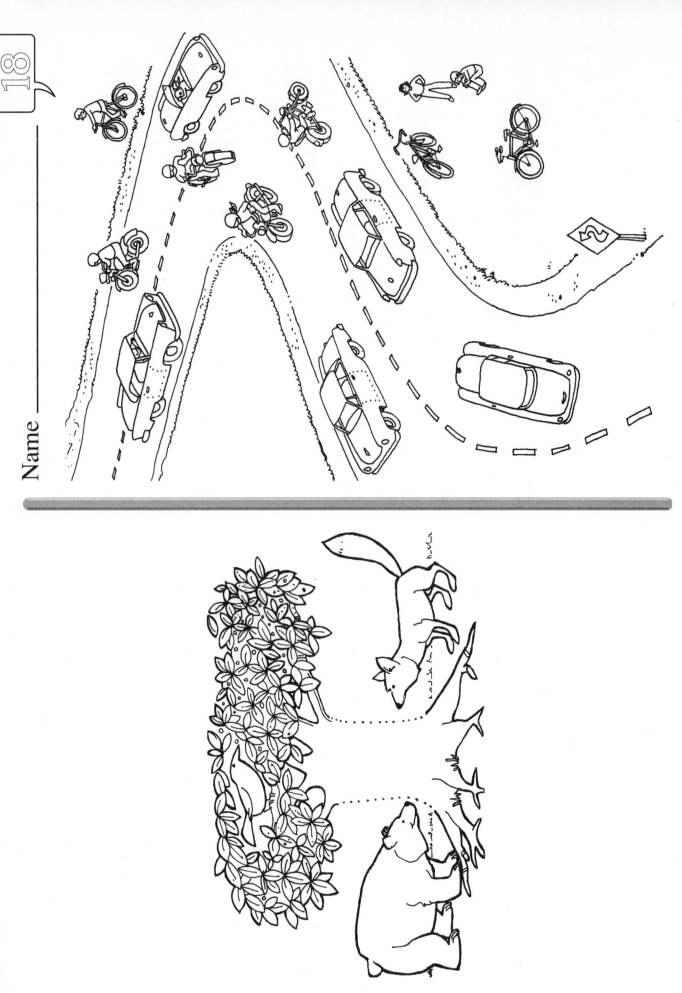

Name _____

Name

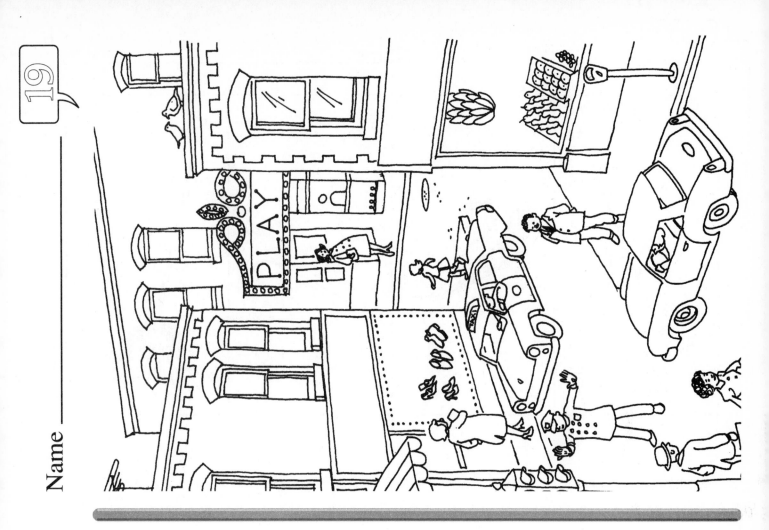

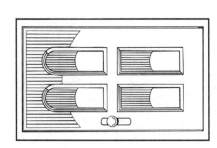

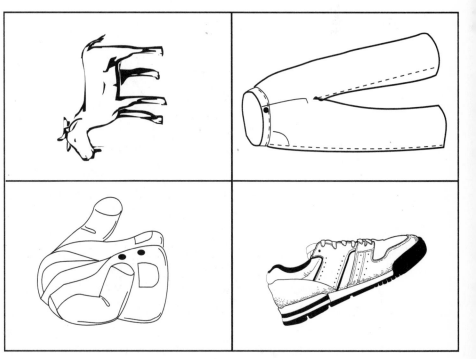

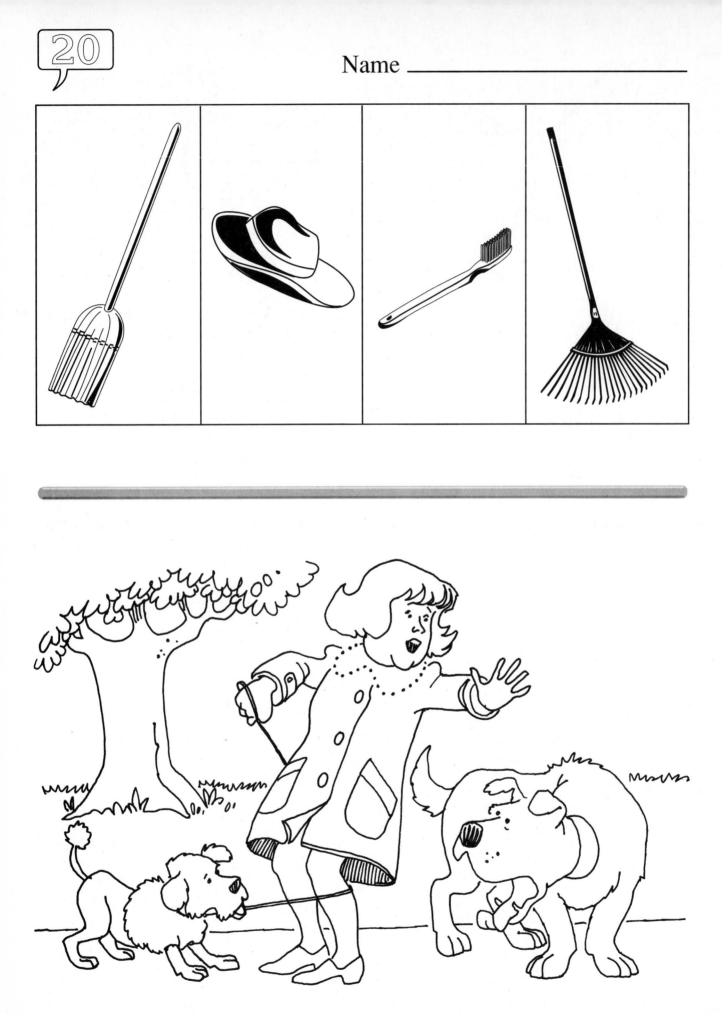

20

Name _____

Name _____

Name _____

Name _____

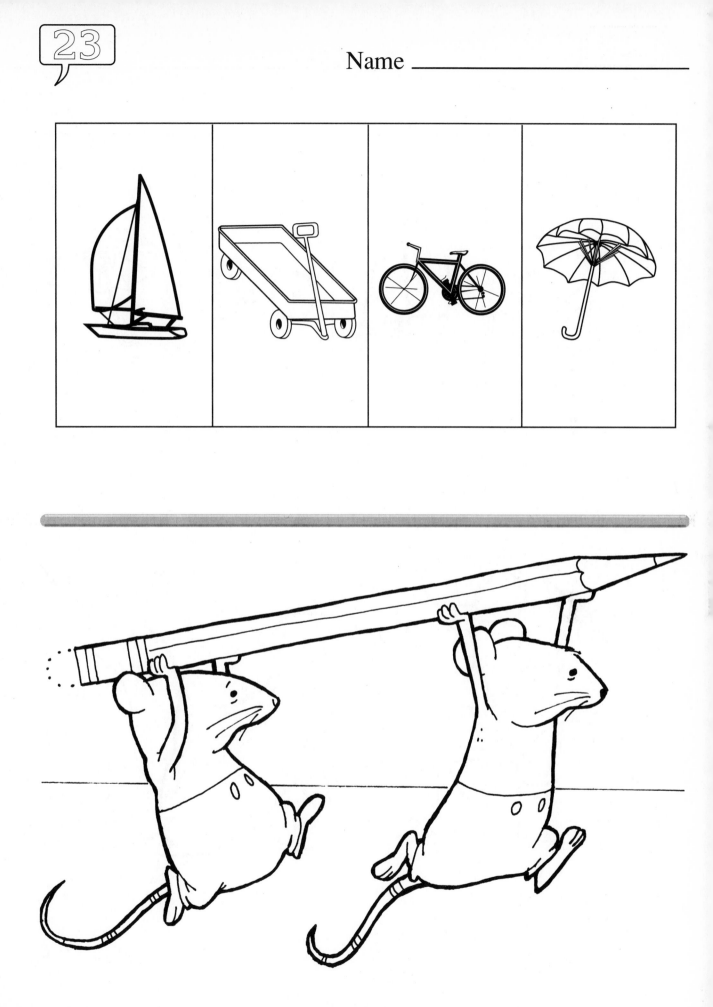

Name _____

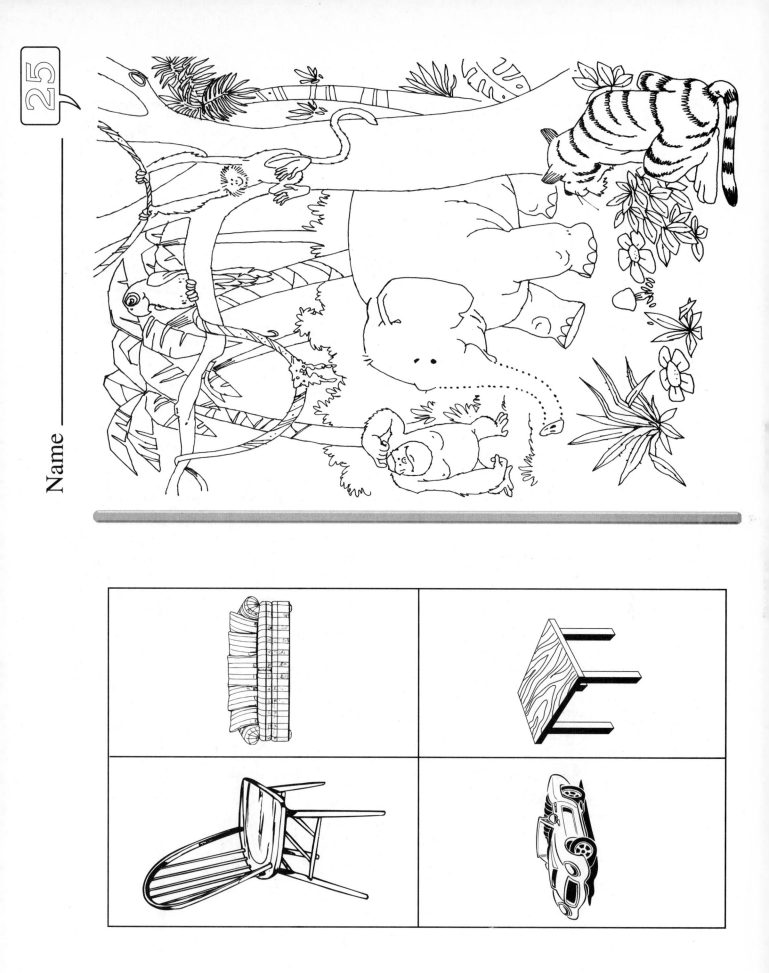

Name

Name _____

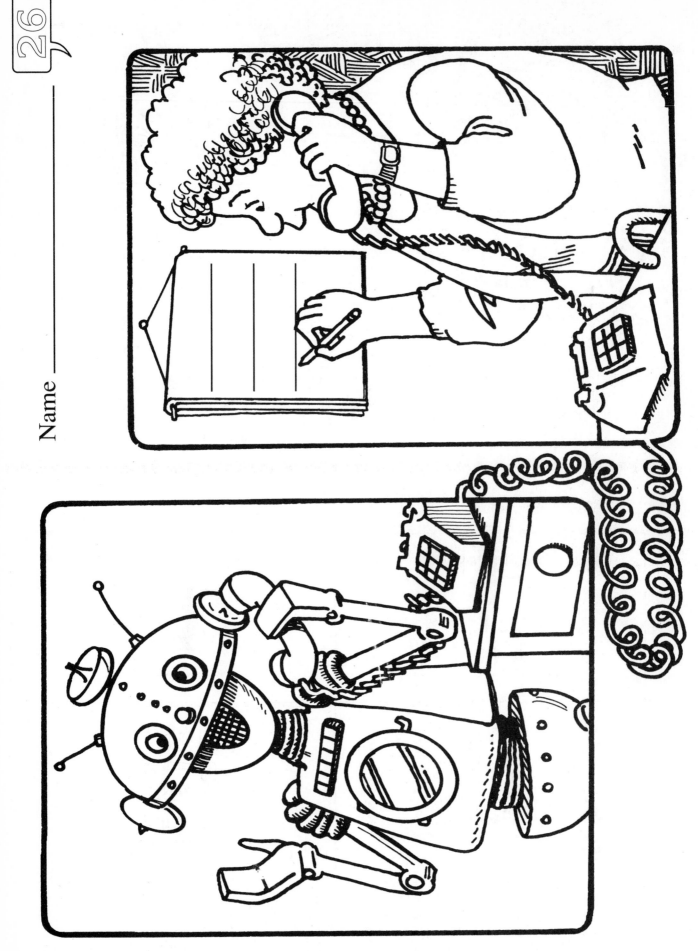

Name _____

27

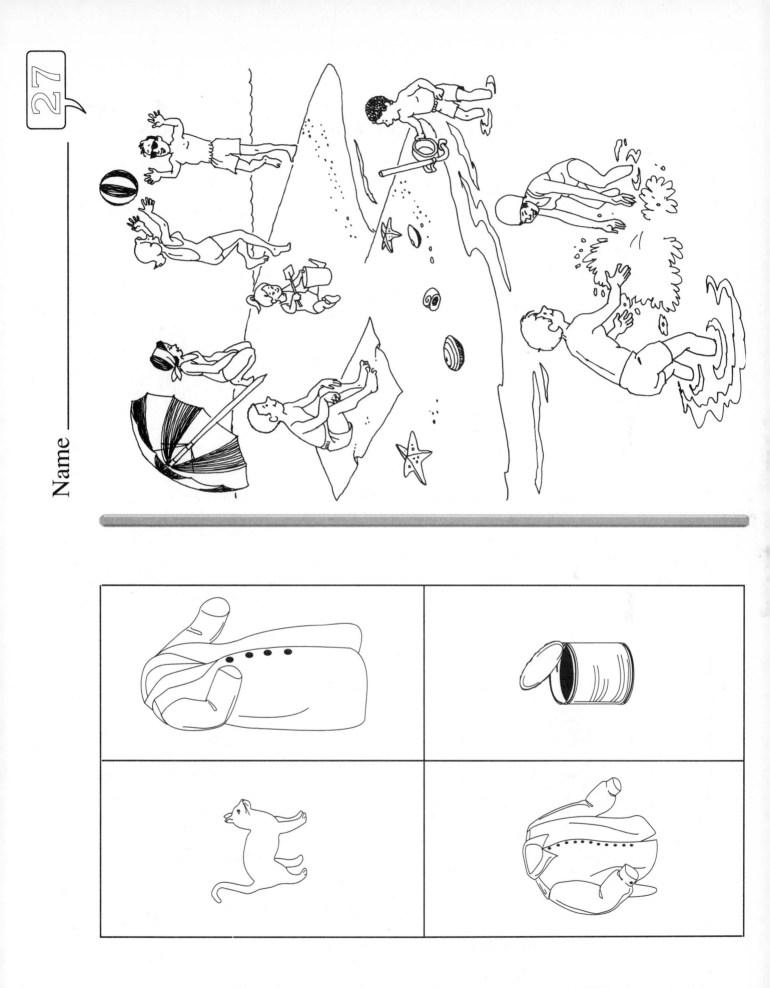

Name _____

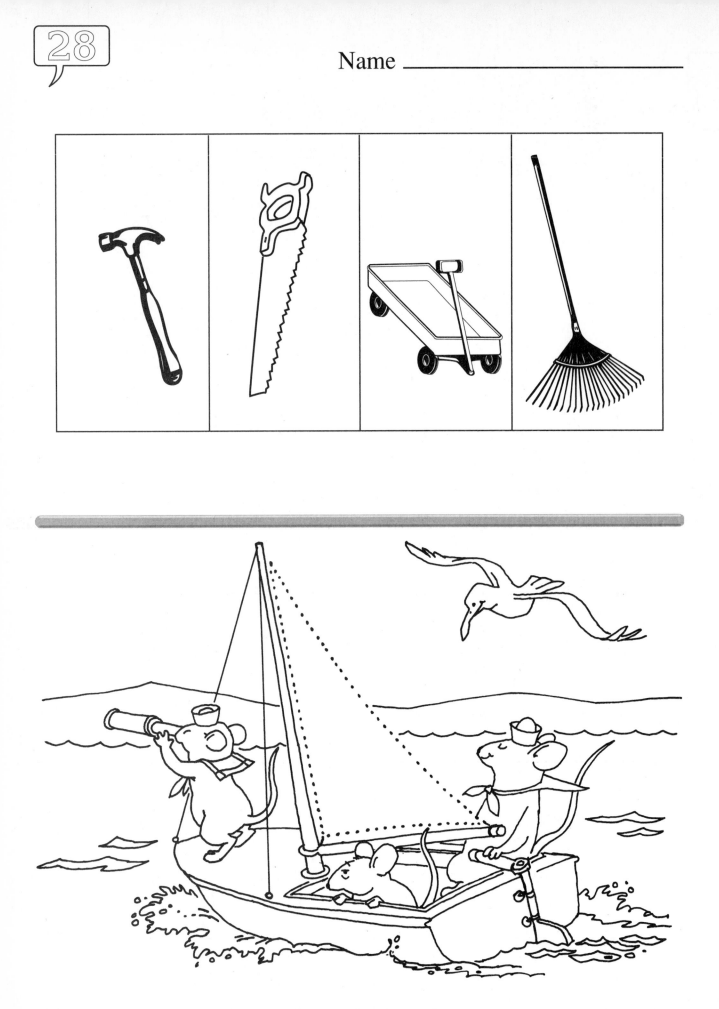

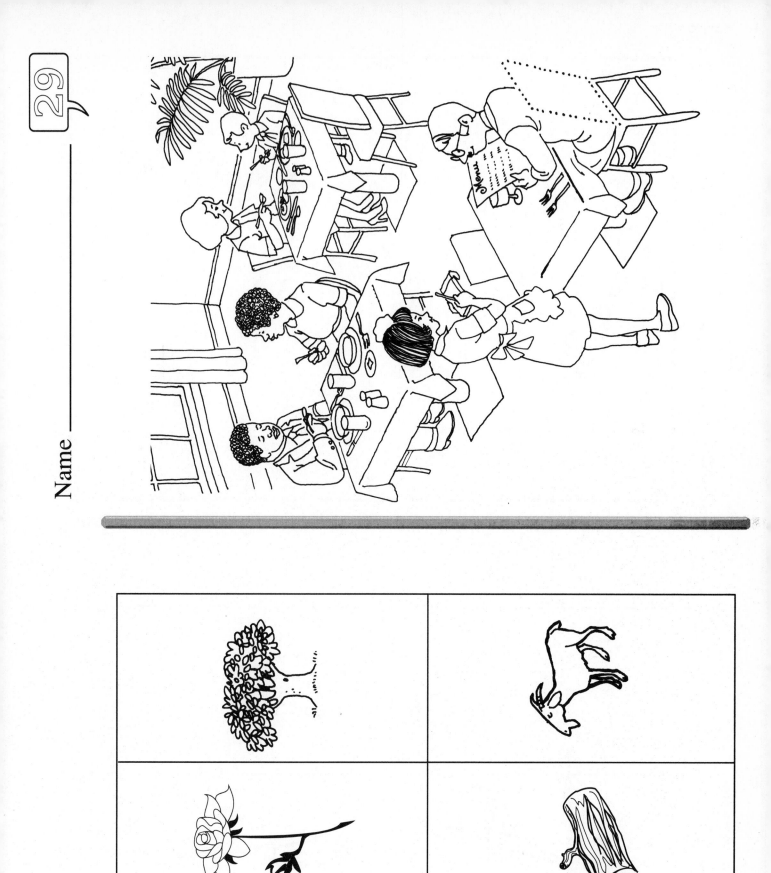

Name _____

29

Name

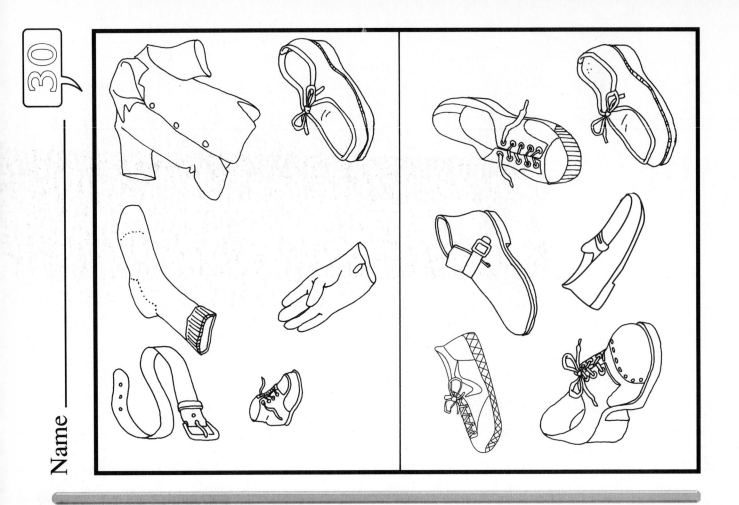

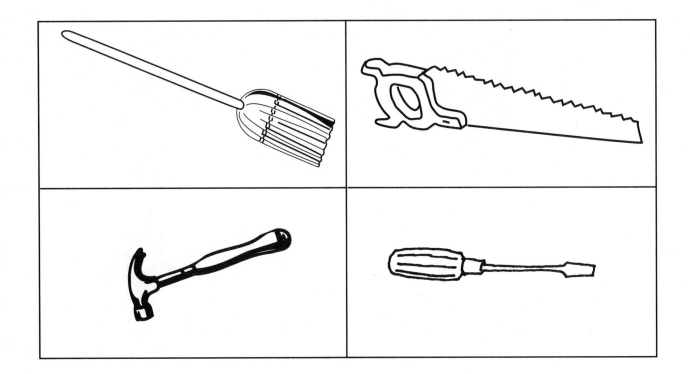

Name _____

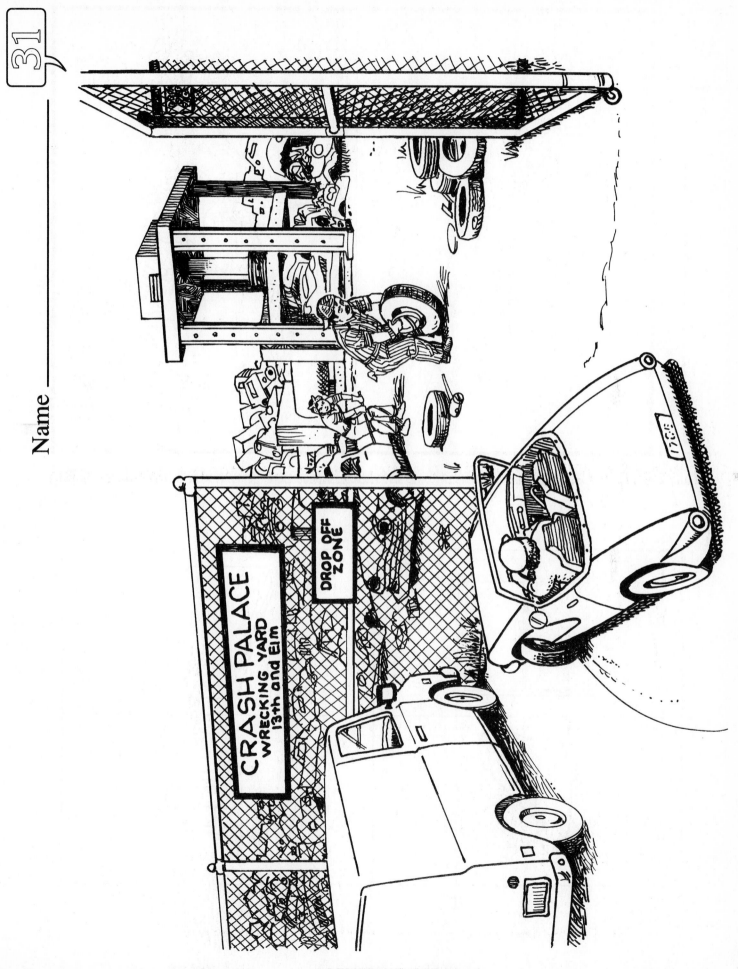

CRASH PALACE
WRECKING YARD
13th and Elm

DROP OFF ZONE

Name

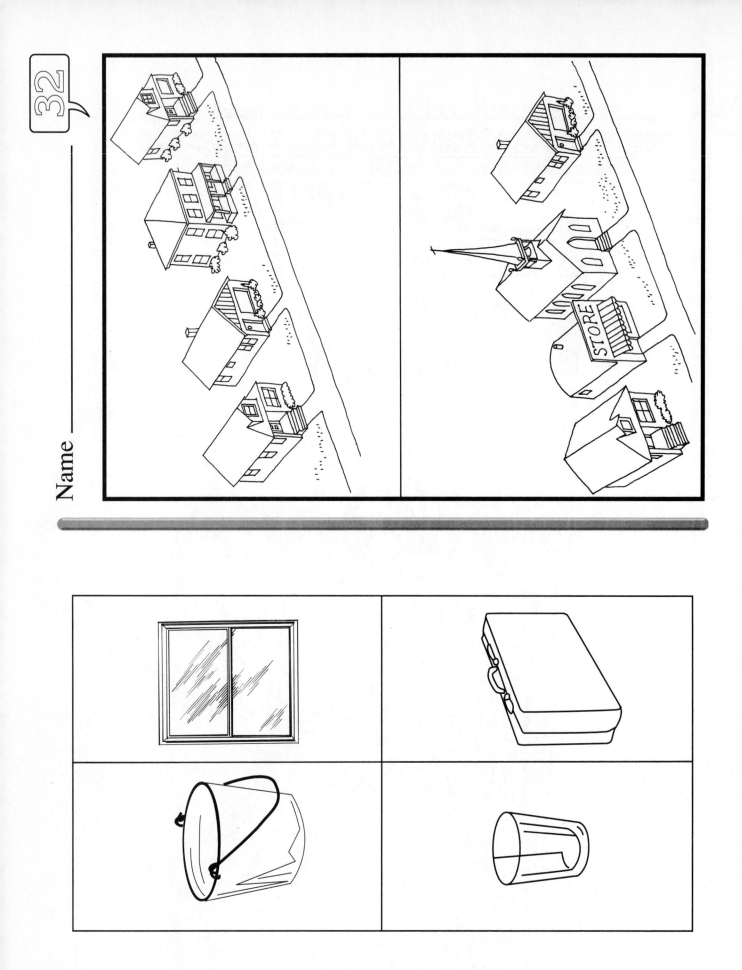

Name _____

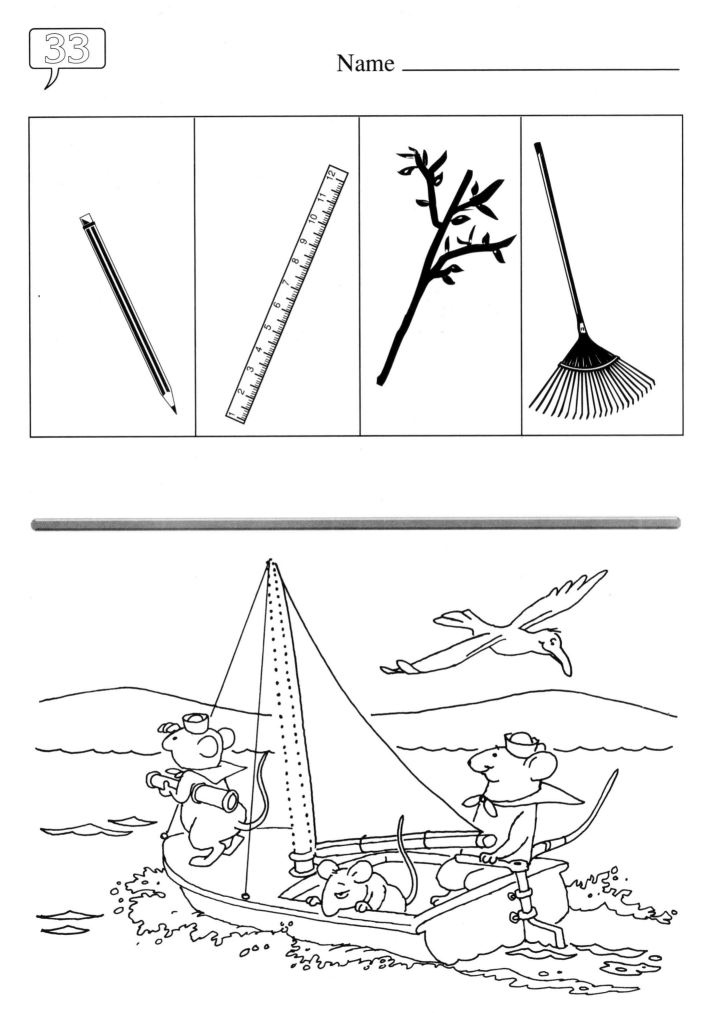

Name _____

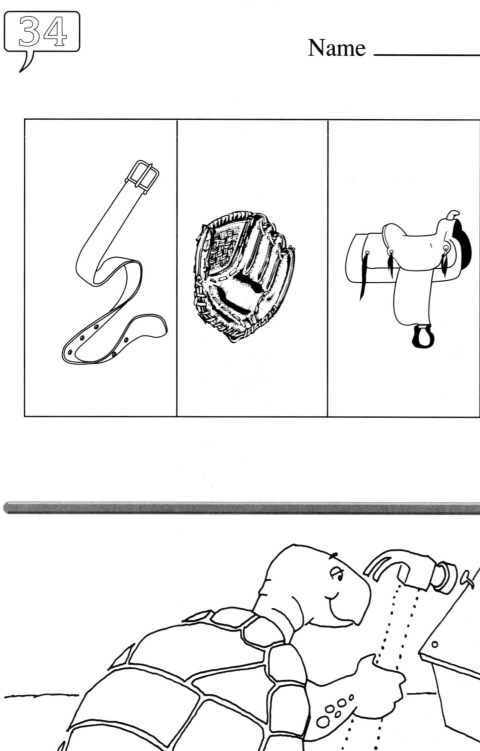

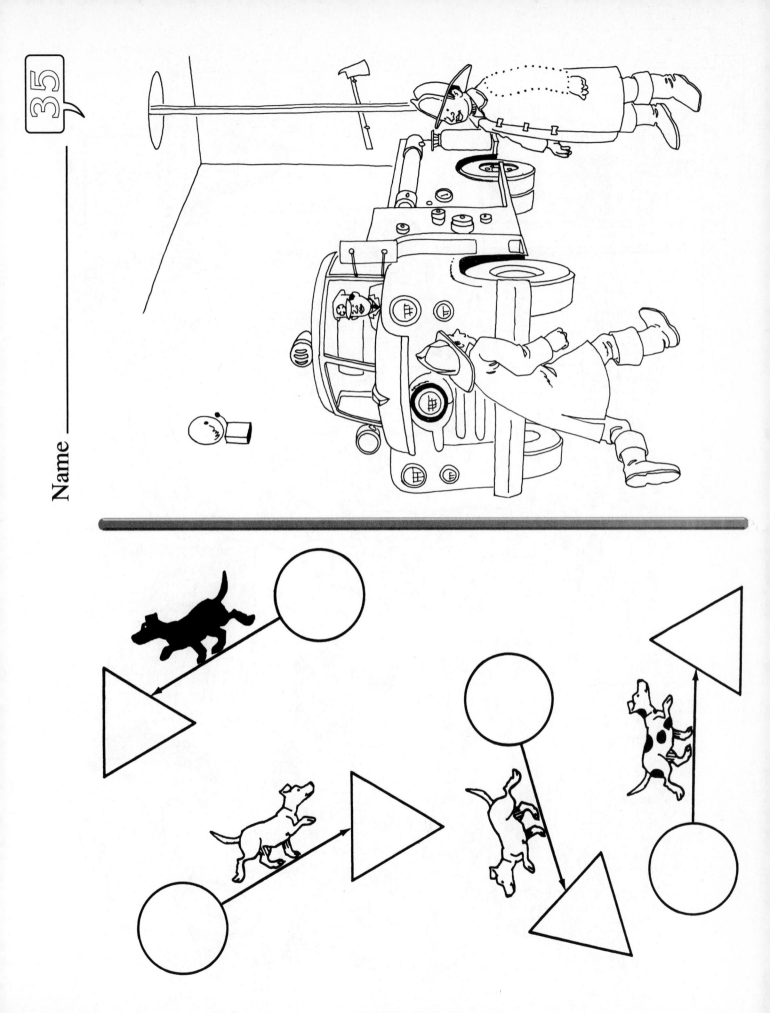

Name _____

35

Name _____

DROP OFF ZONE

Name _____

Name _____

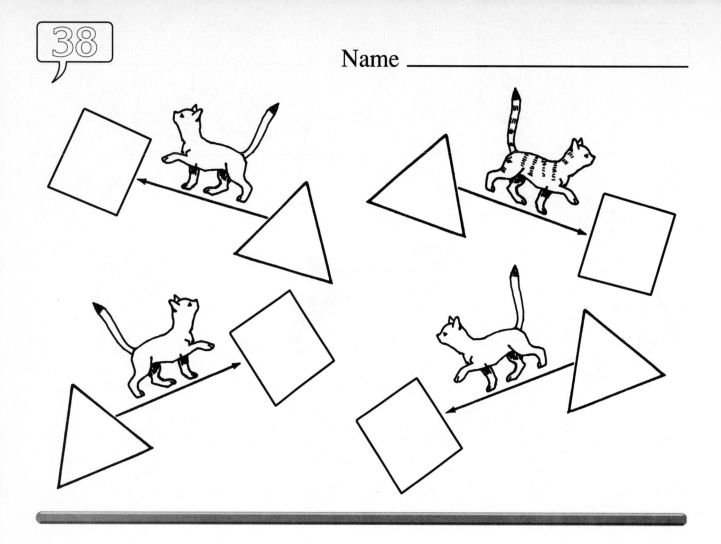

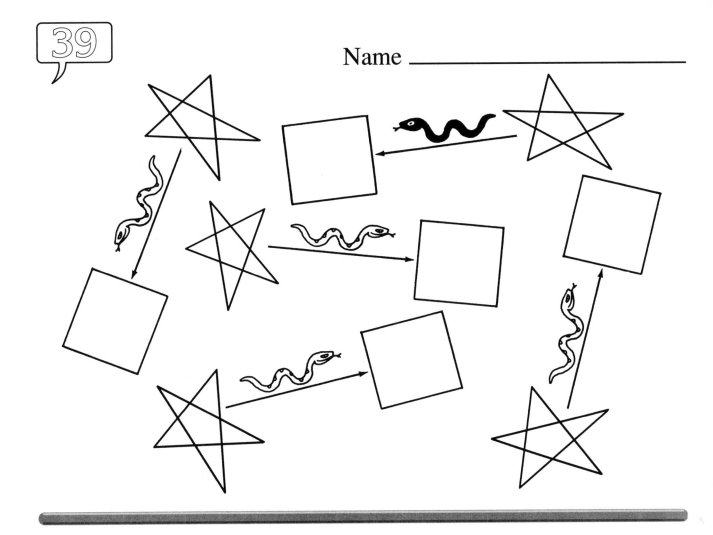

Name _____

40

Name

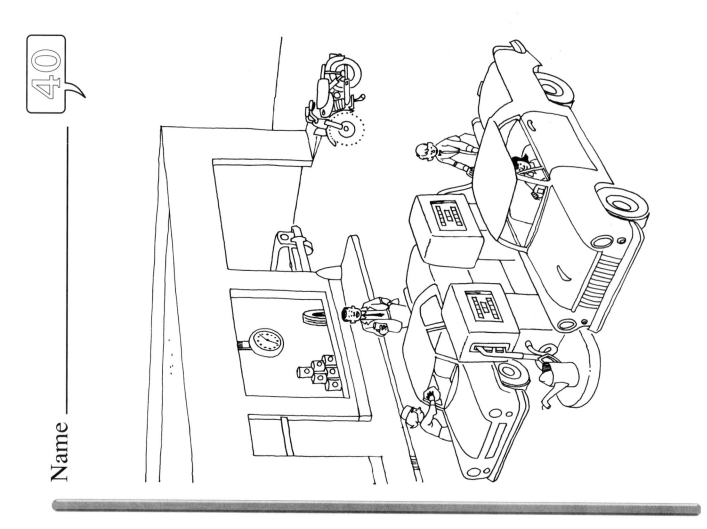

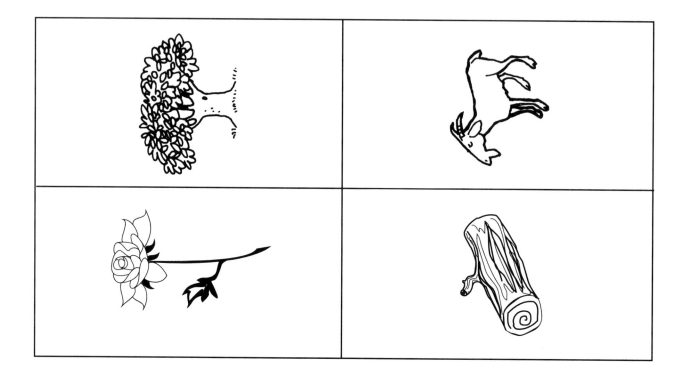

Name _____

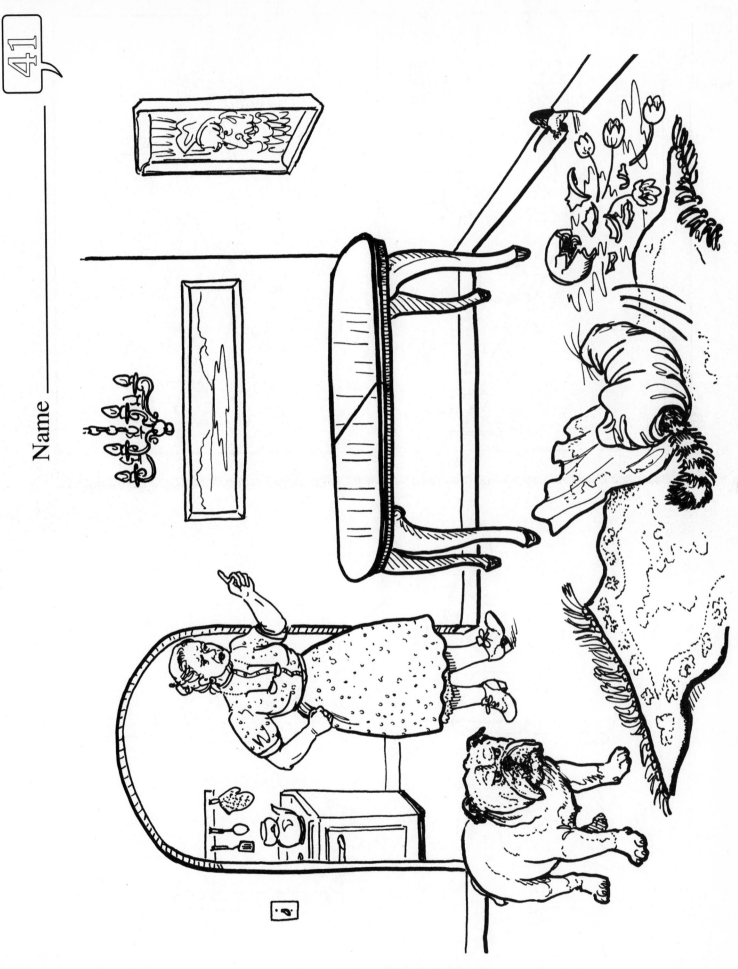

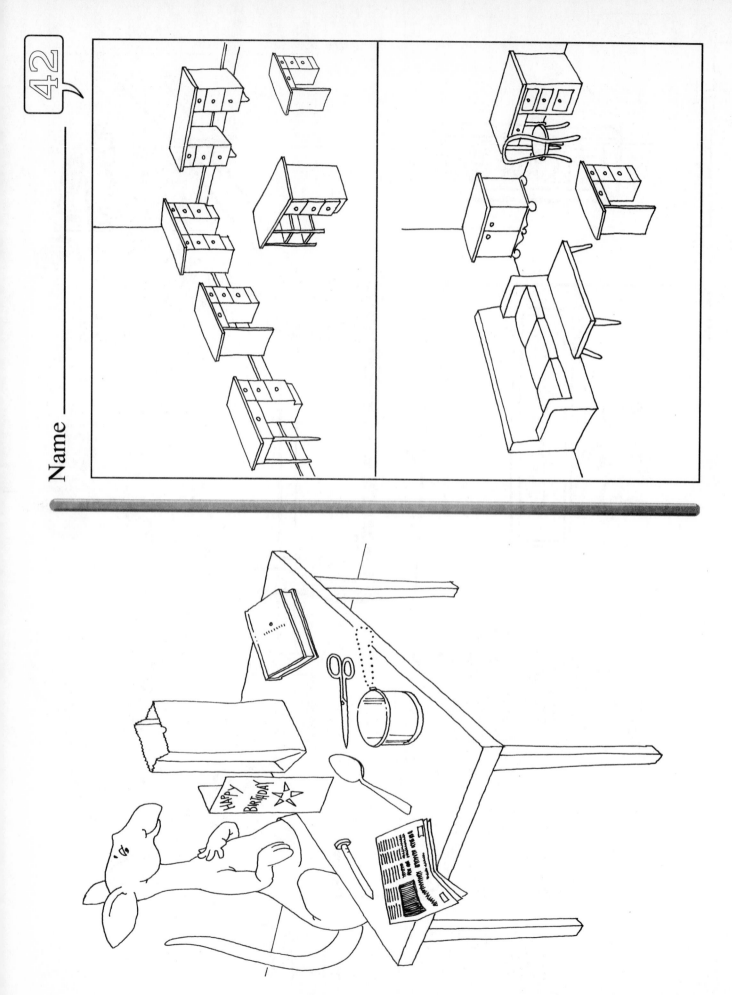

Name _____

Name _____

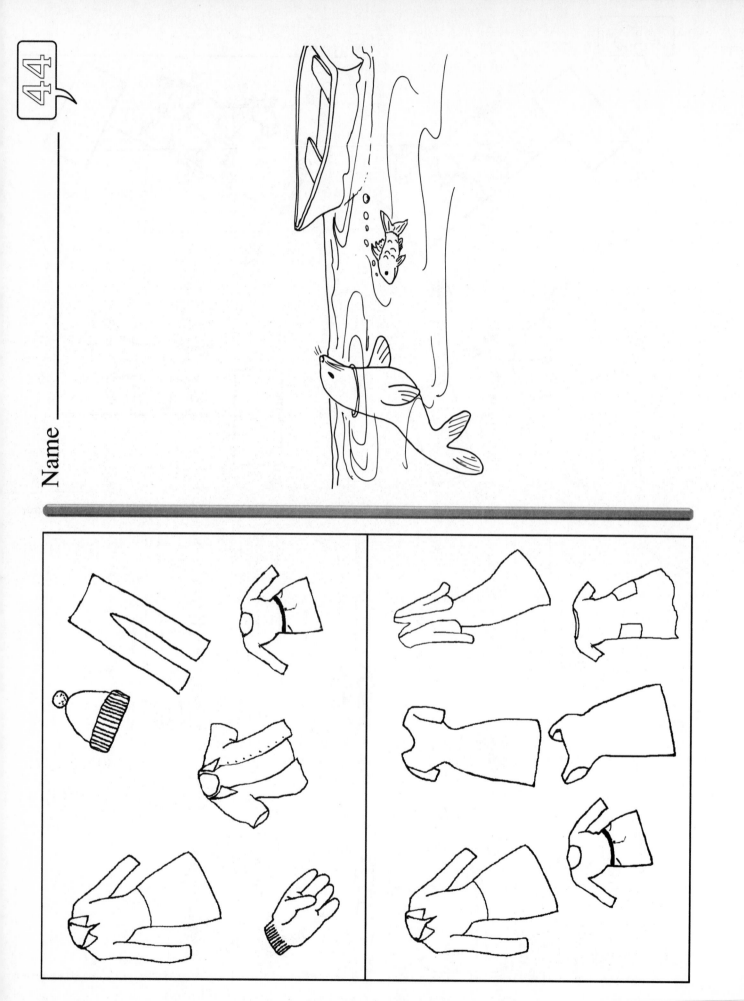

Name _____

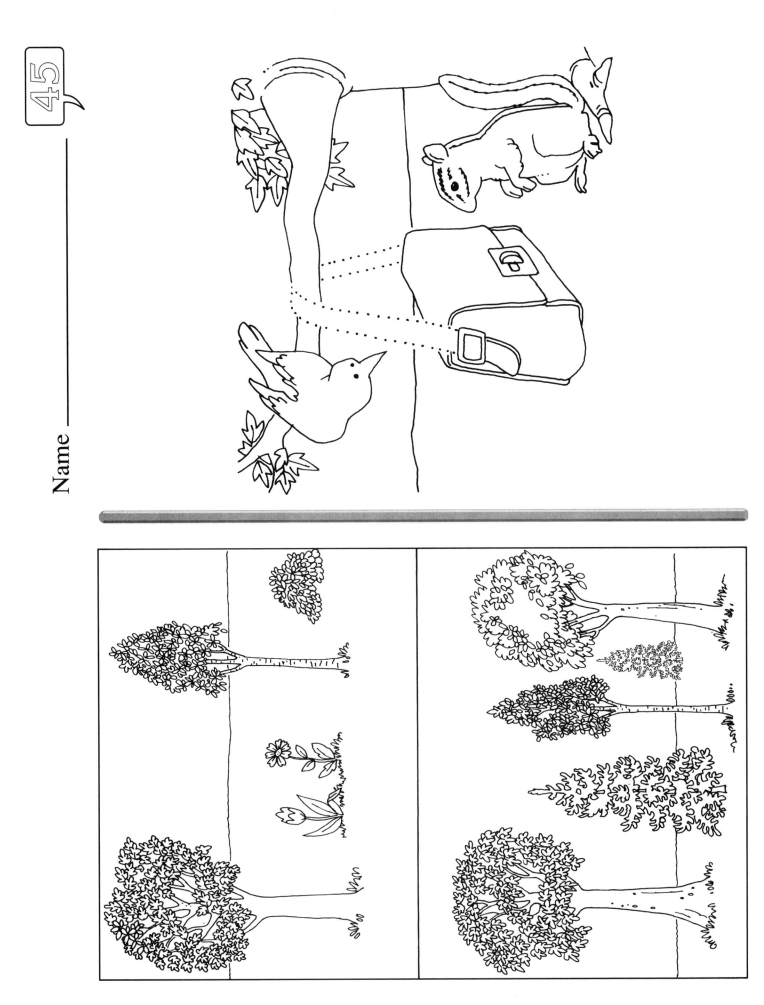

Name

45

Name

Name

Name _____

48

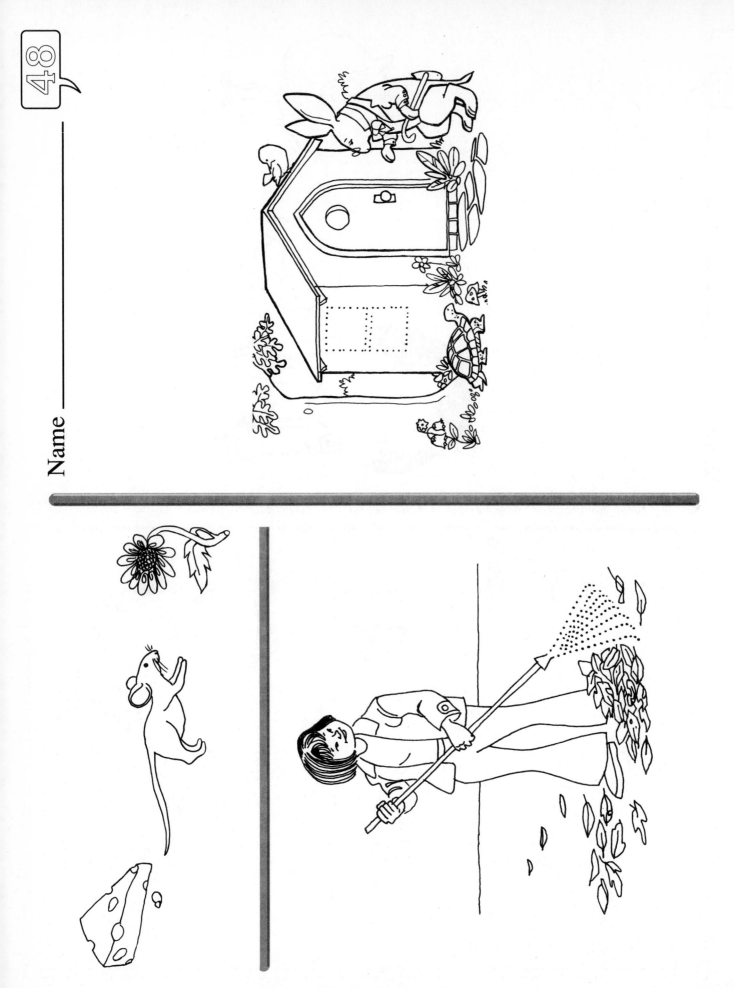

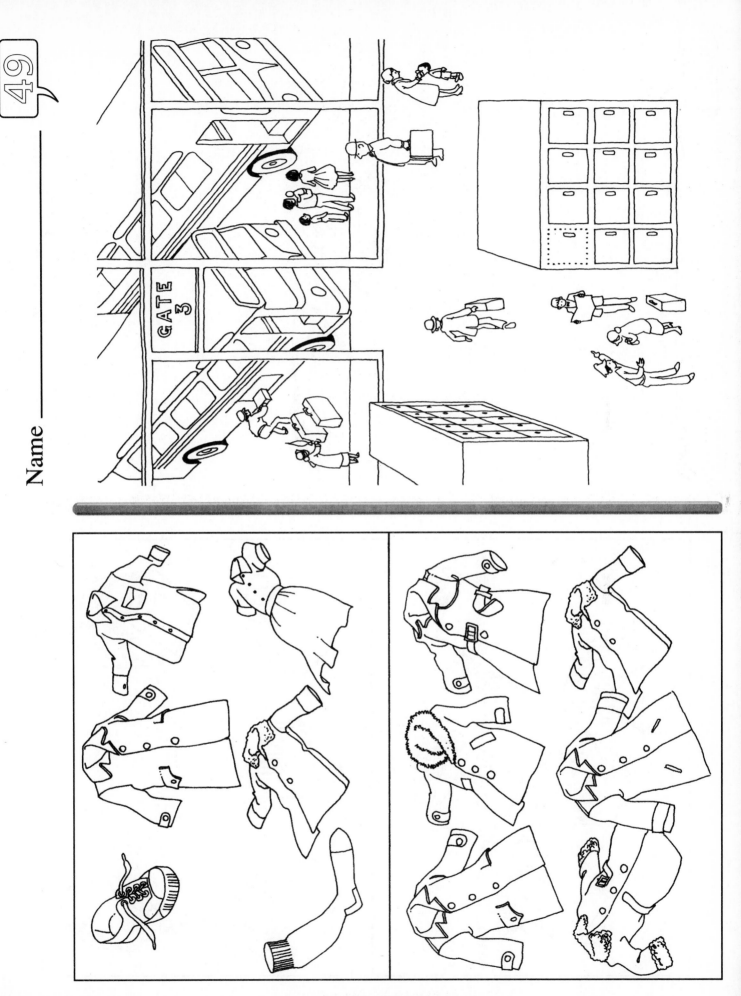

49

Name _____

Name _____

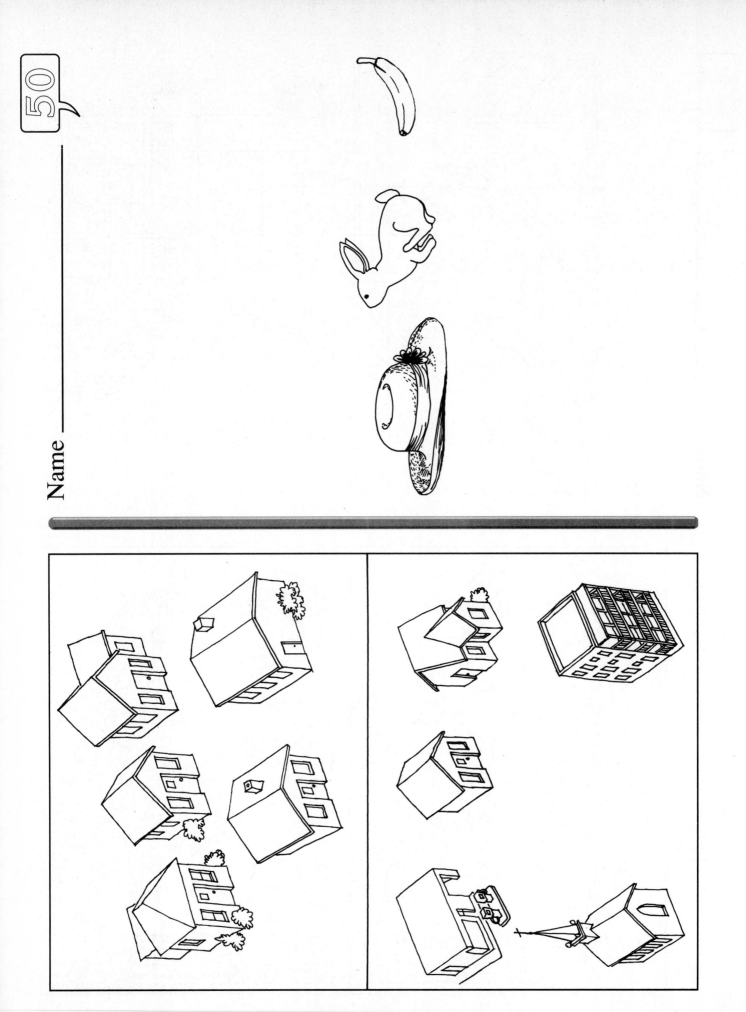

Name _____

Name

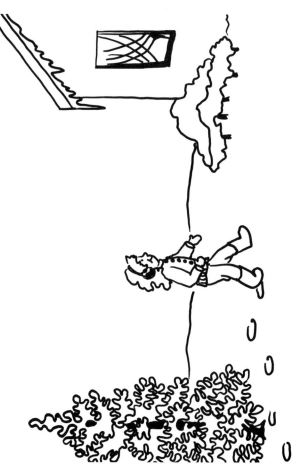

Name

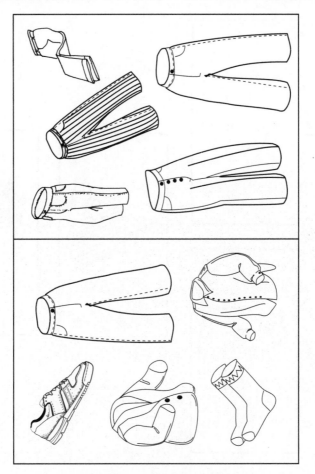

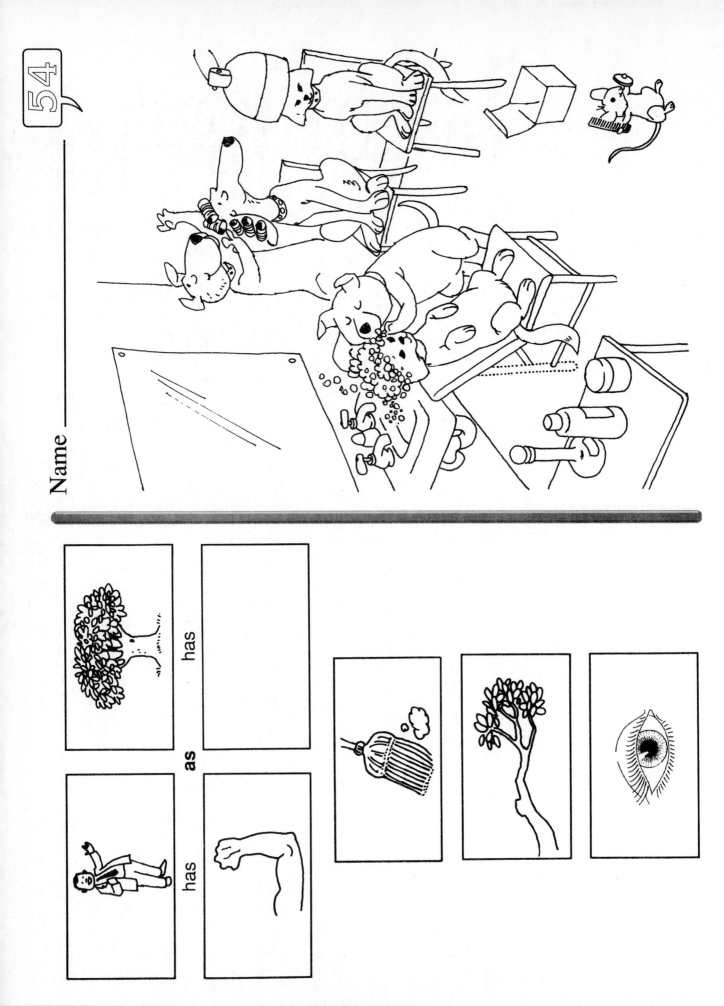

54

Name

as   has   has

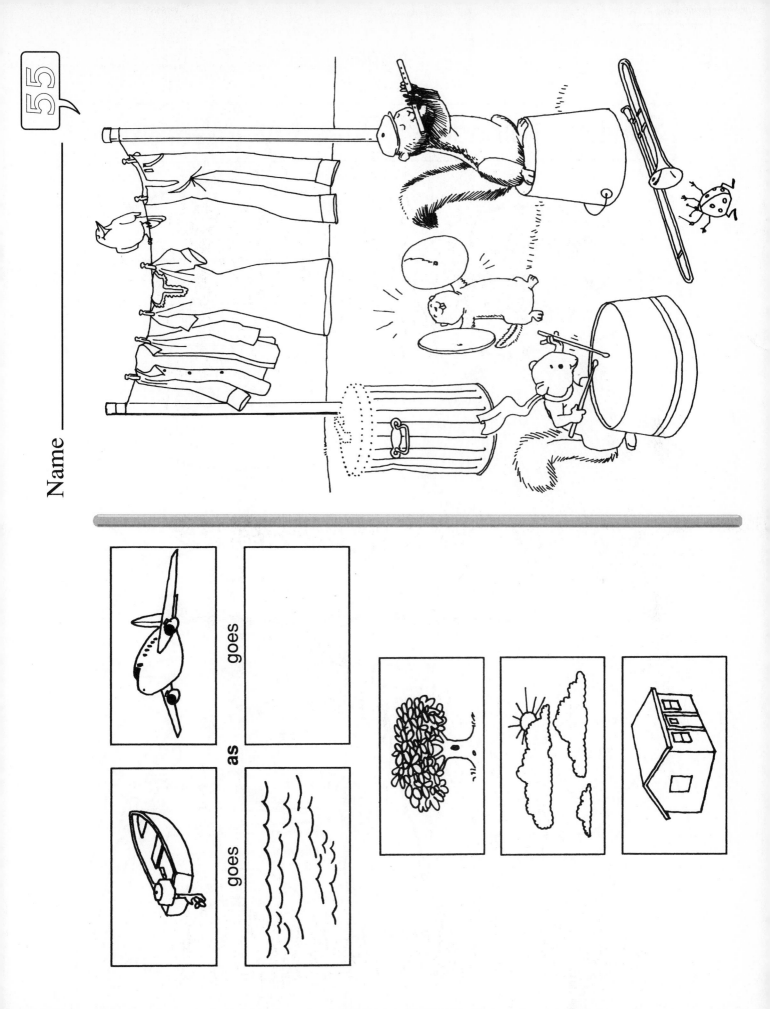

Name

55

goes

as

goes

Name _____

| Sunday | Monday | Tuesday | Wednesday |

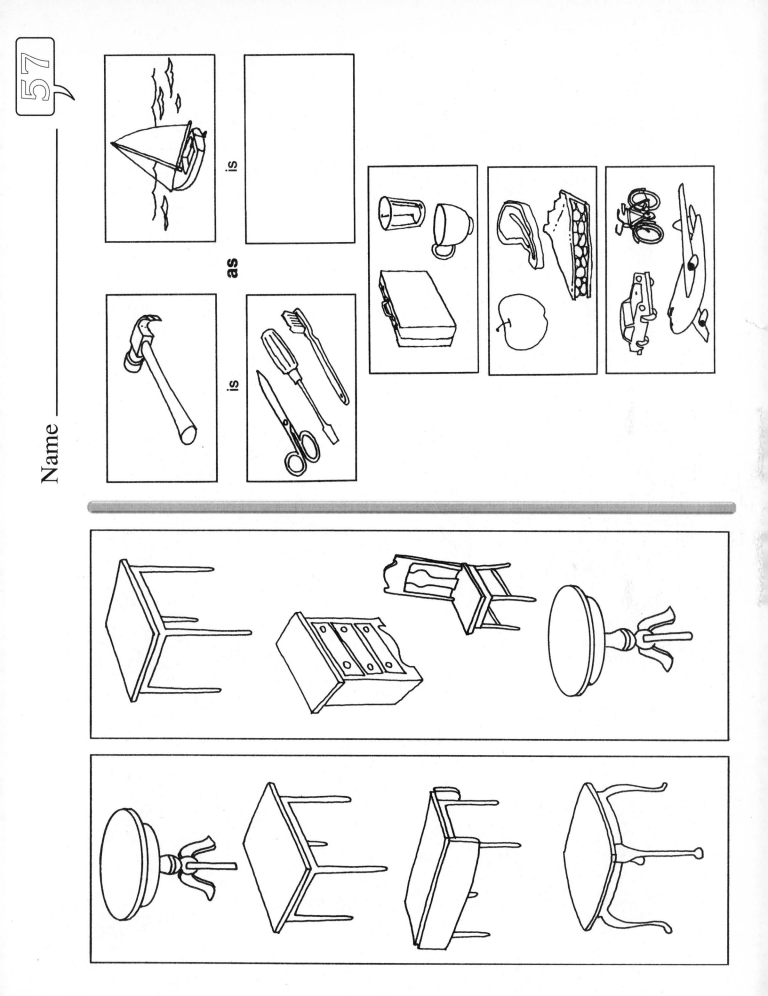

Name

is

as

is

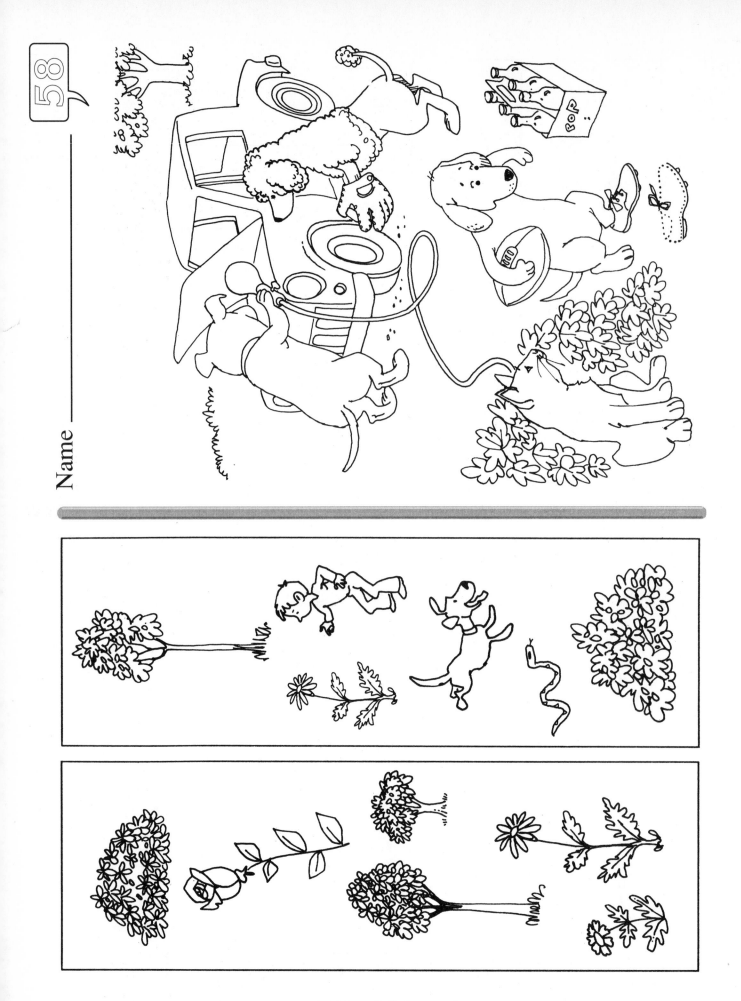

58

Name

59

Name _____

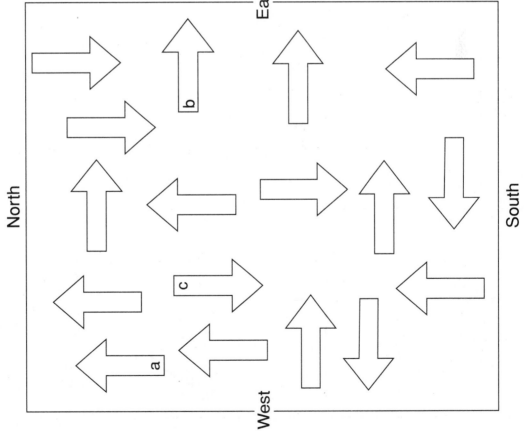

East

North

South

West

b

c

a

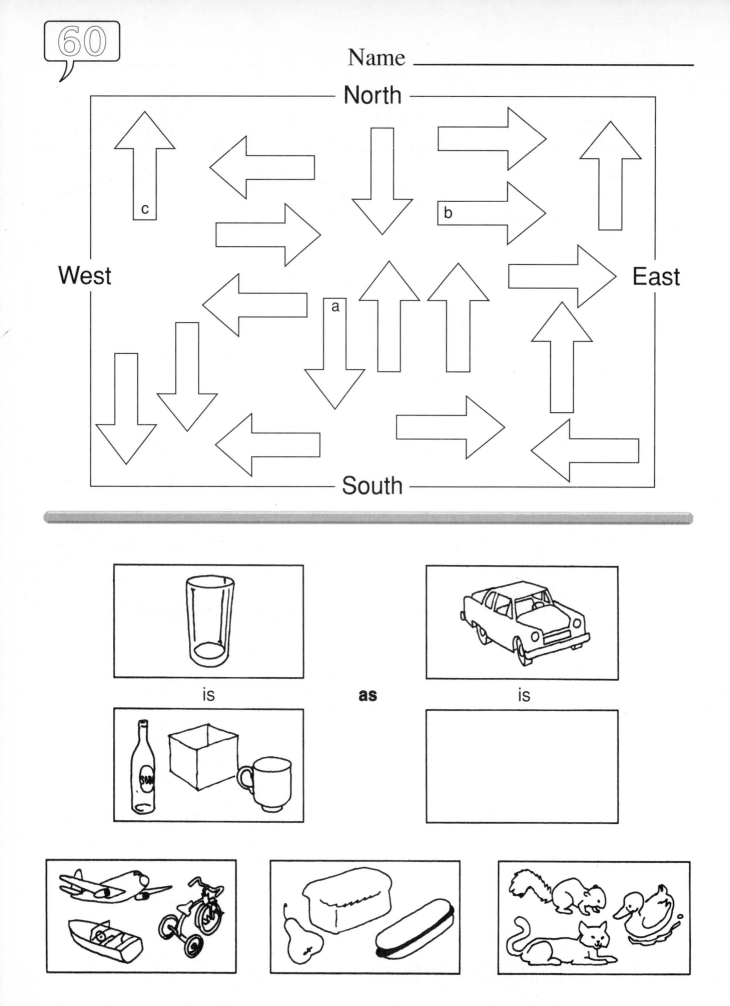

60

Name _____

North

West

East

c

b

a

South

is   **as**   is

Name _____

| Wednesday | Thursday | Friday | Saturday |

Wow, you can say ALL the days of the week!

Sunday, Monday, Tuesday,

_____,

_____,

_____,

_____.

Name _____

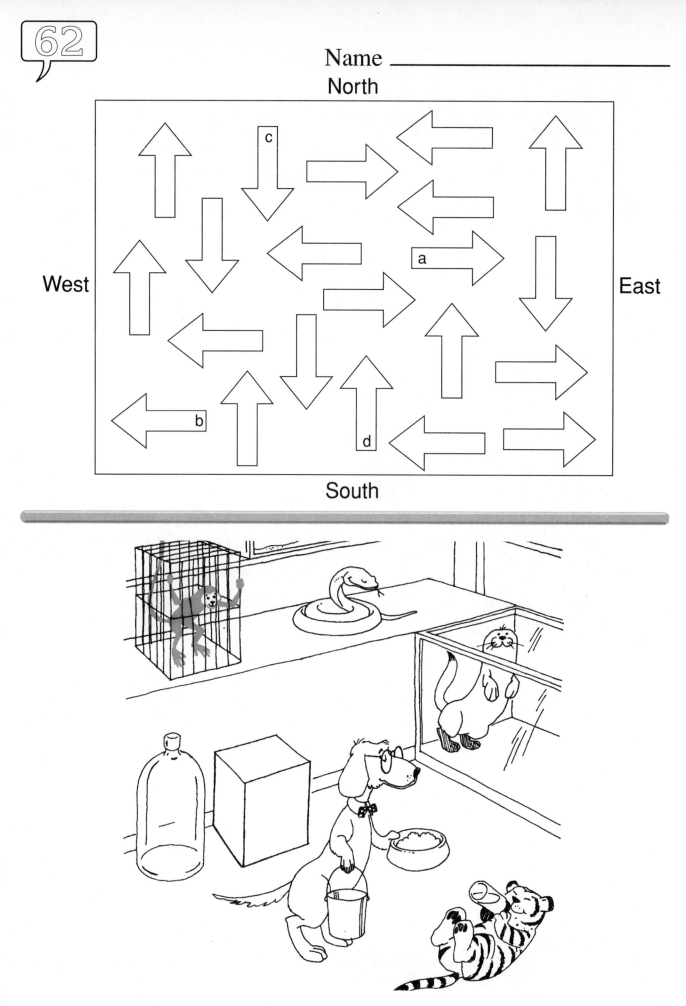

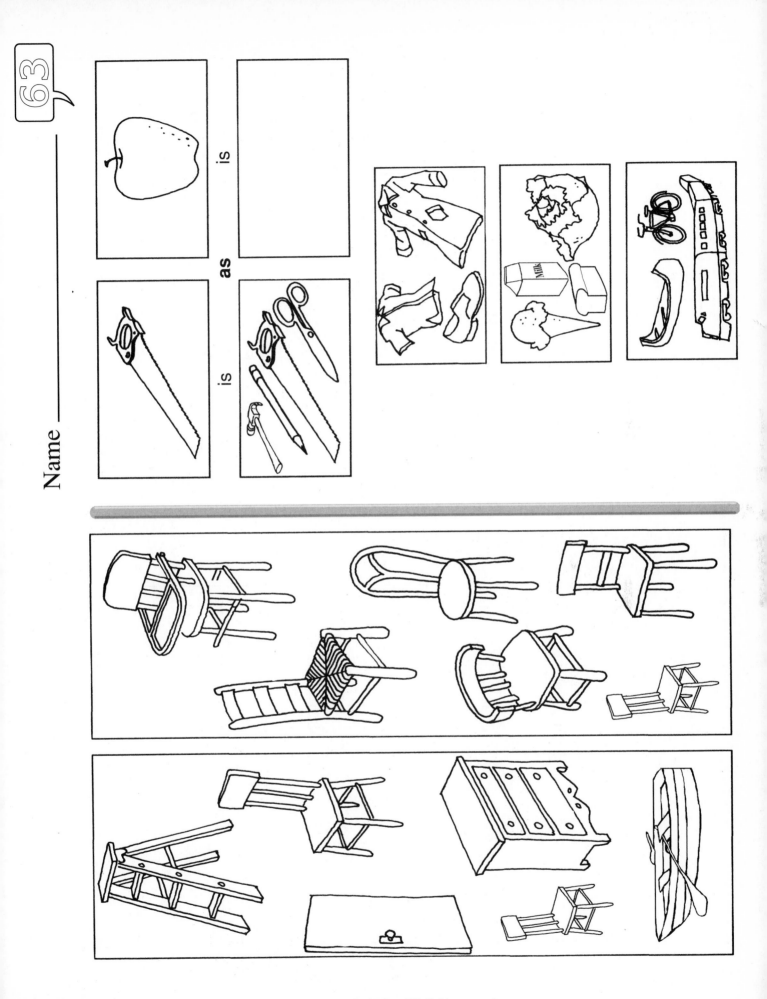

Name _____

63

is

as

is

Milk

Name _____

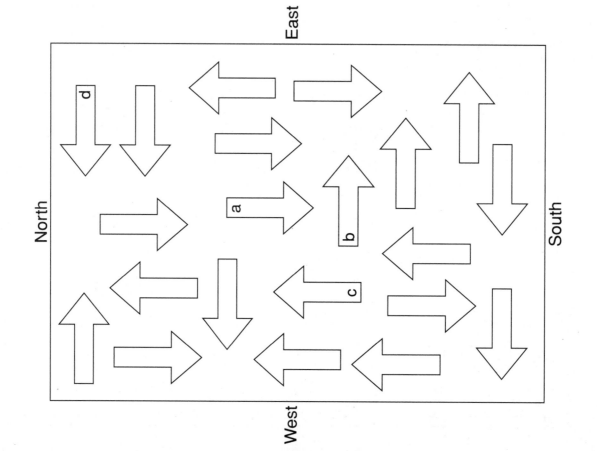

East

North

South

West

d

a

b

c

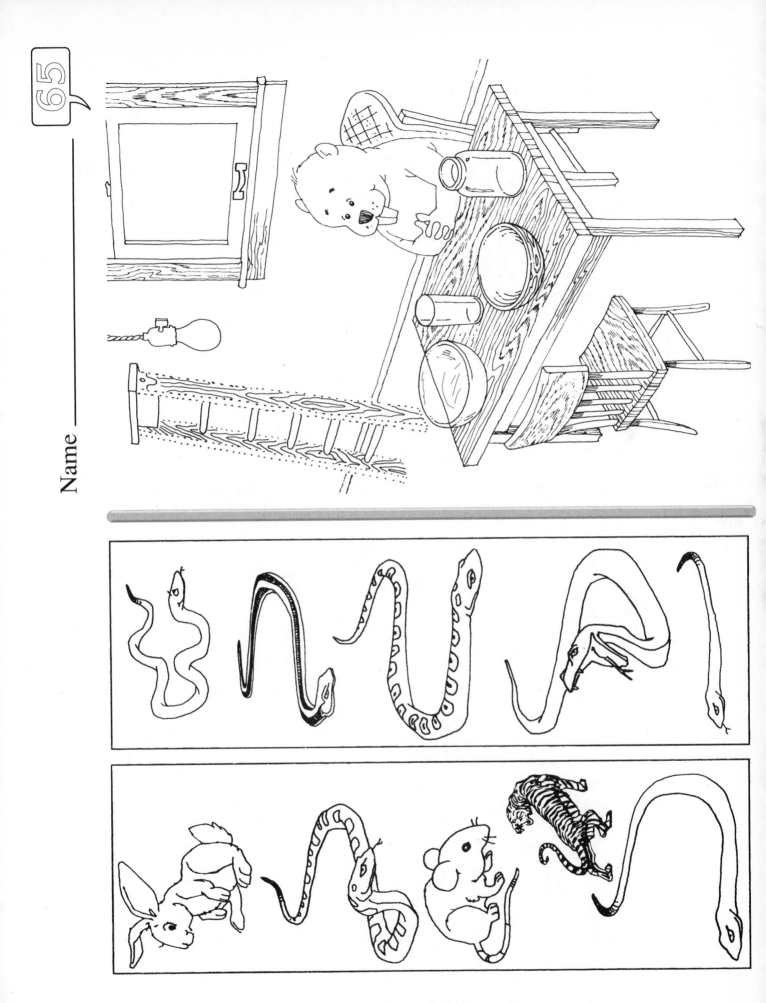

65

Name

Name

67

Name

is

as

is

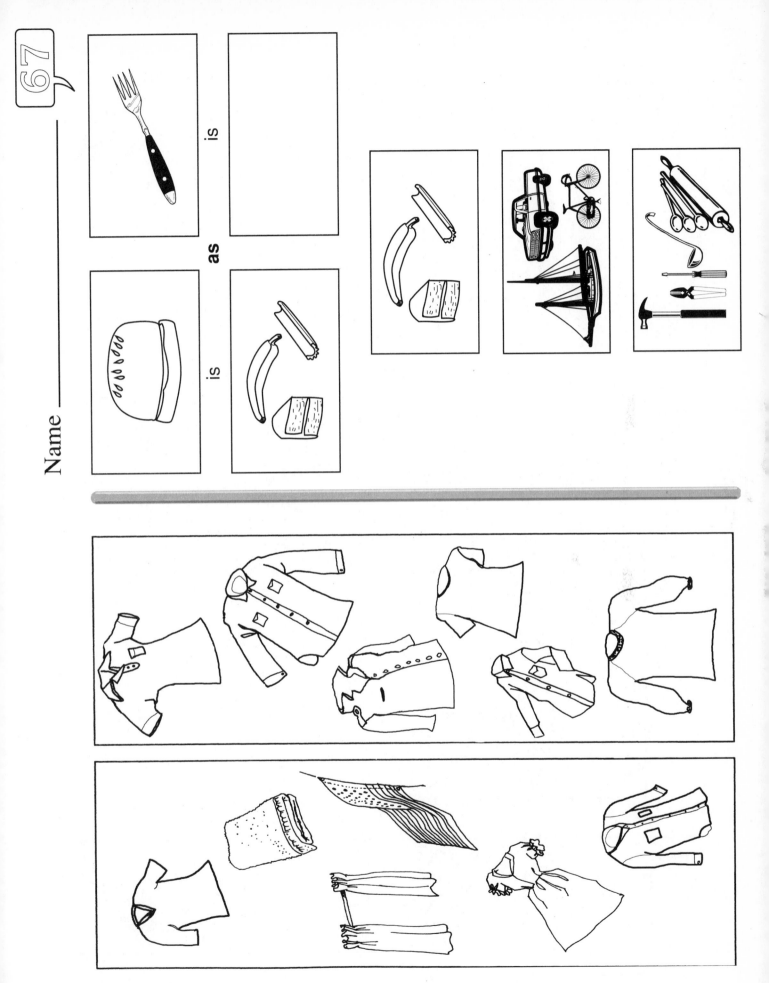

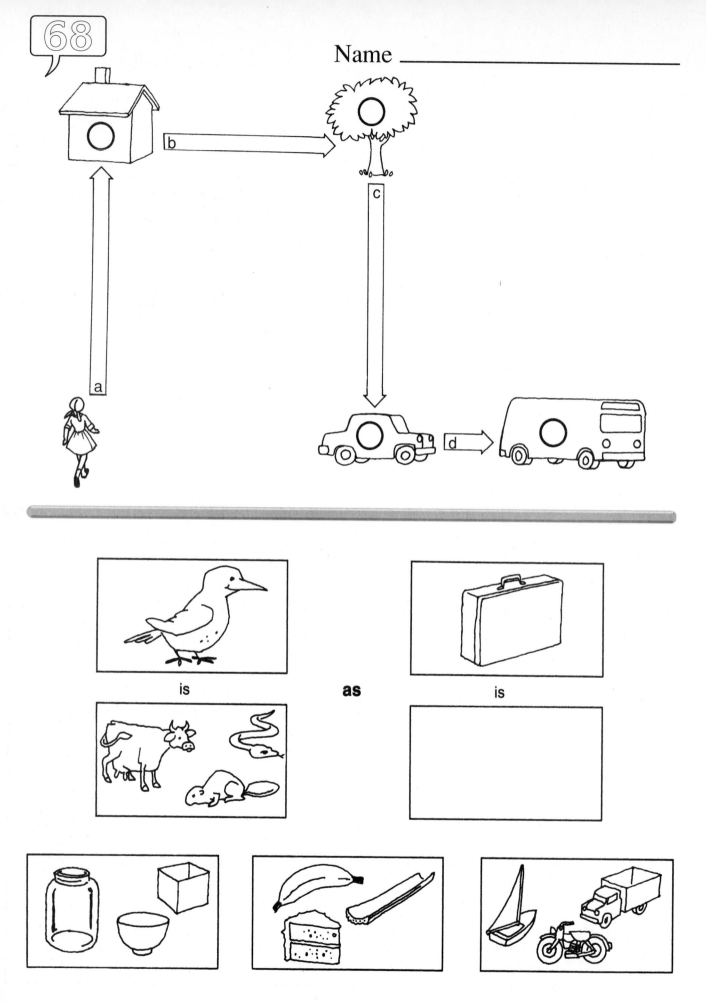

68

Name _____

is   **as**   is

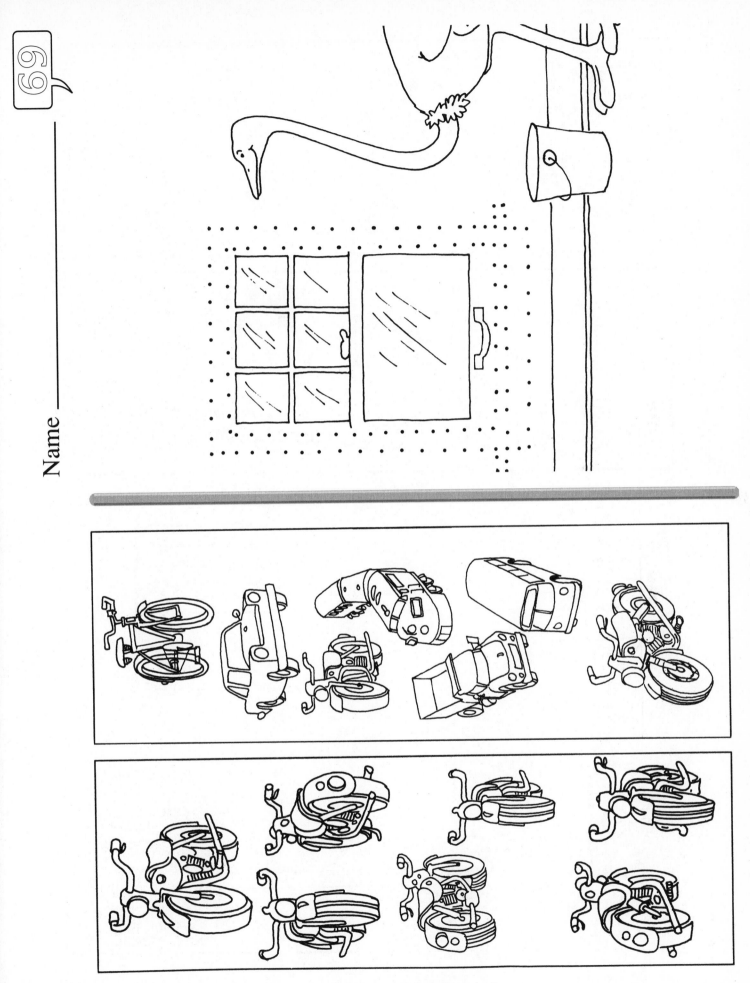

Name _____

69

70

Name

Name _____

Name

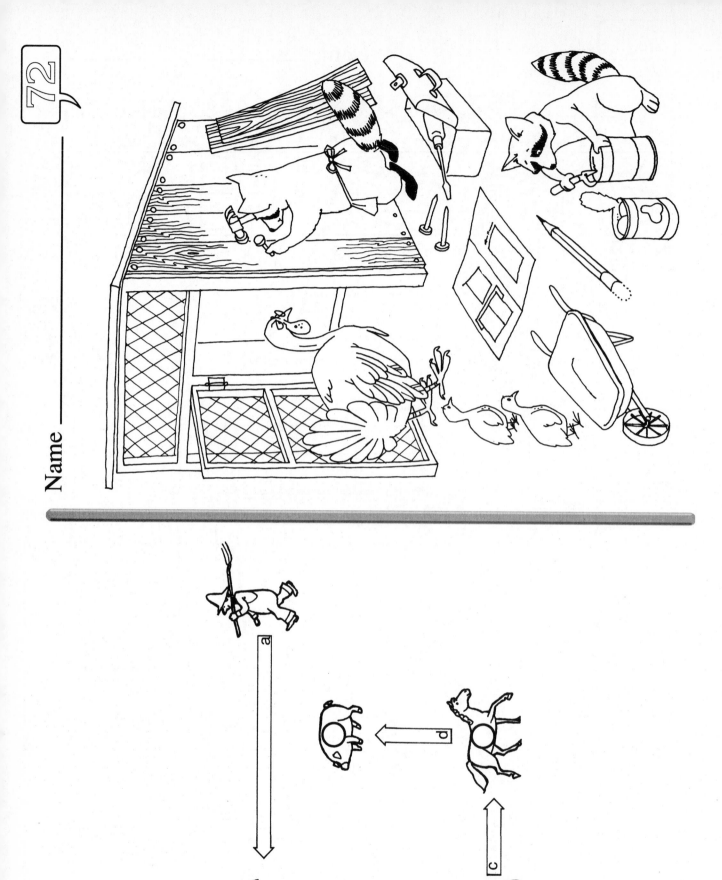

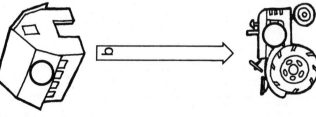

Name _____

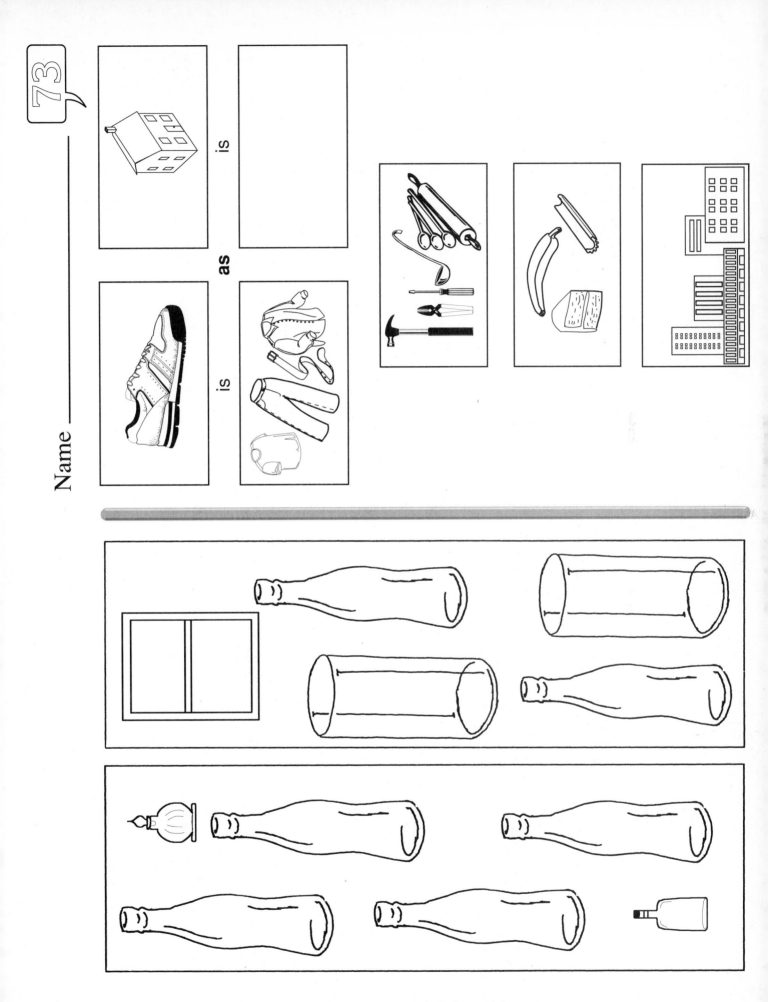

is

as

is

Name _____

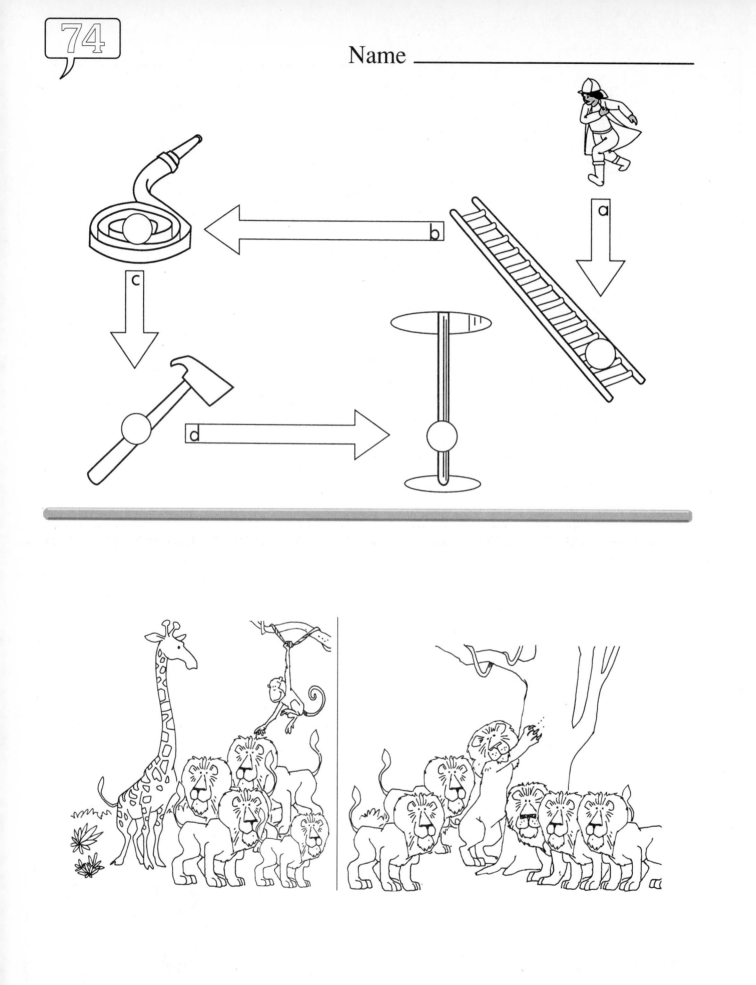

75

Name _____

is   as   is

© SRA/McGraw-Hill. All rights reserved.

Name _____

1. _____

2. _____

3. _____

4. _____

5. _____

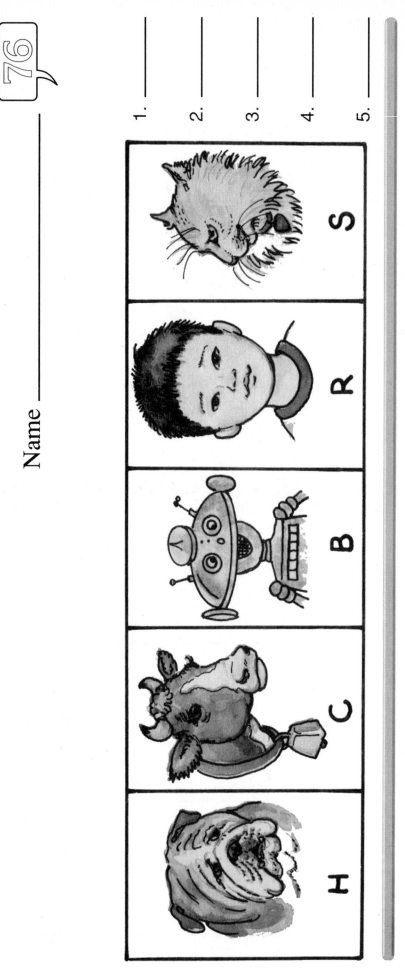

S

R

B

C

H

1.

2.

3.

4.

Name _____

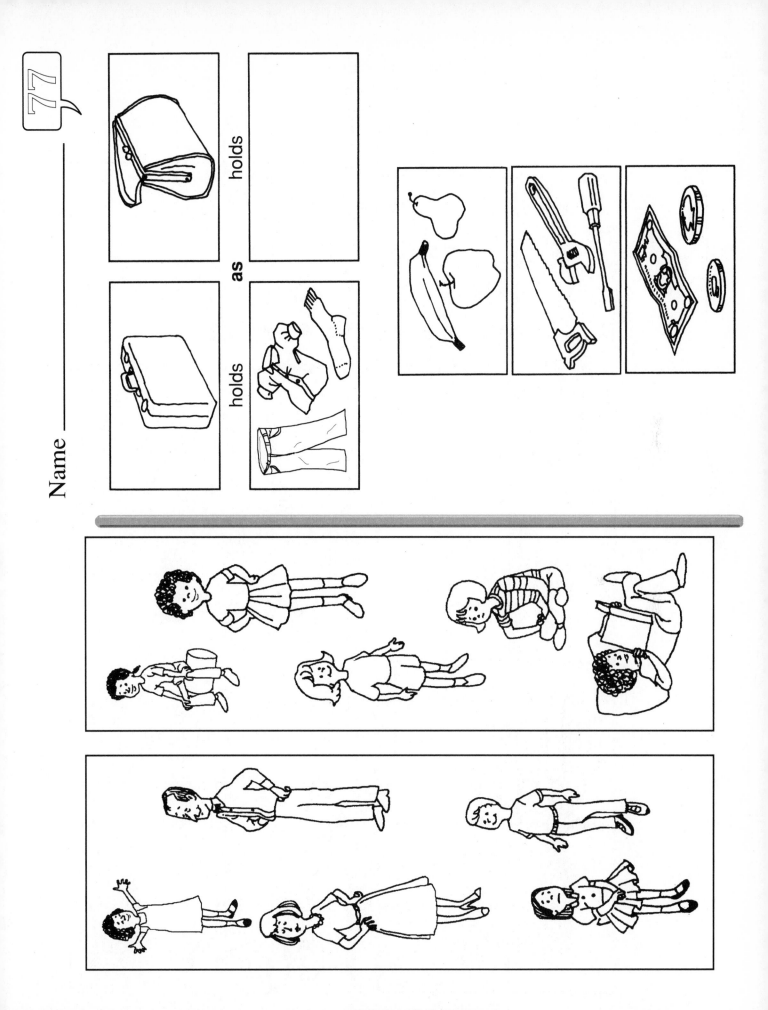

holds   as   holds

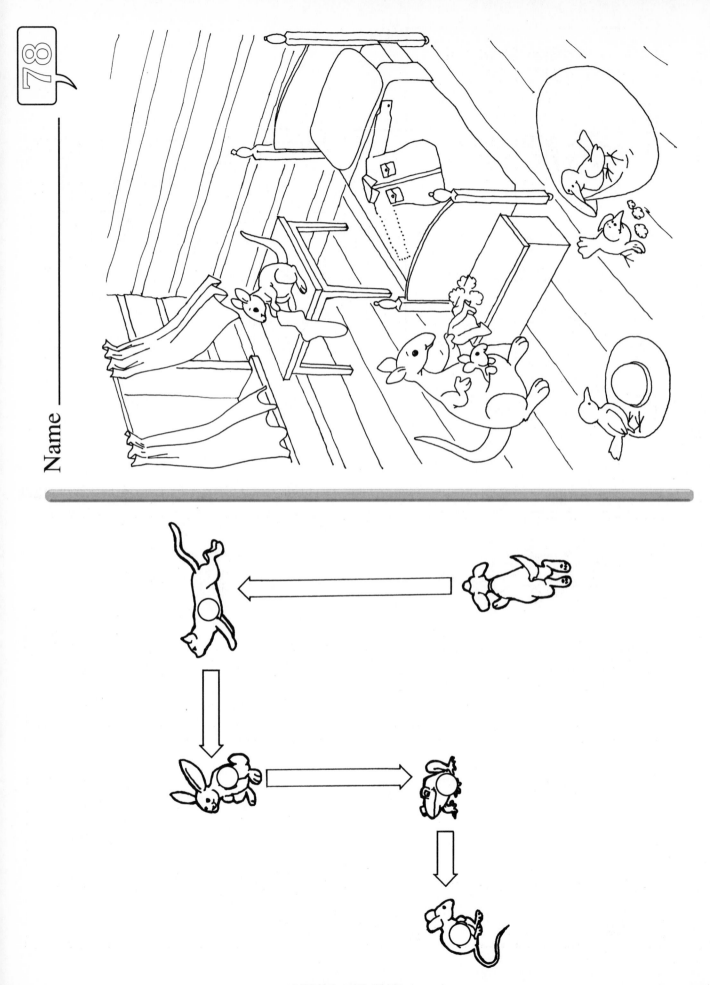

Name _____

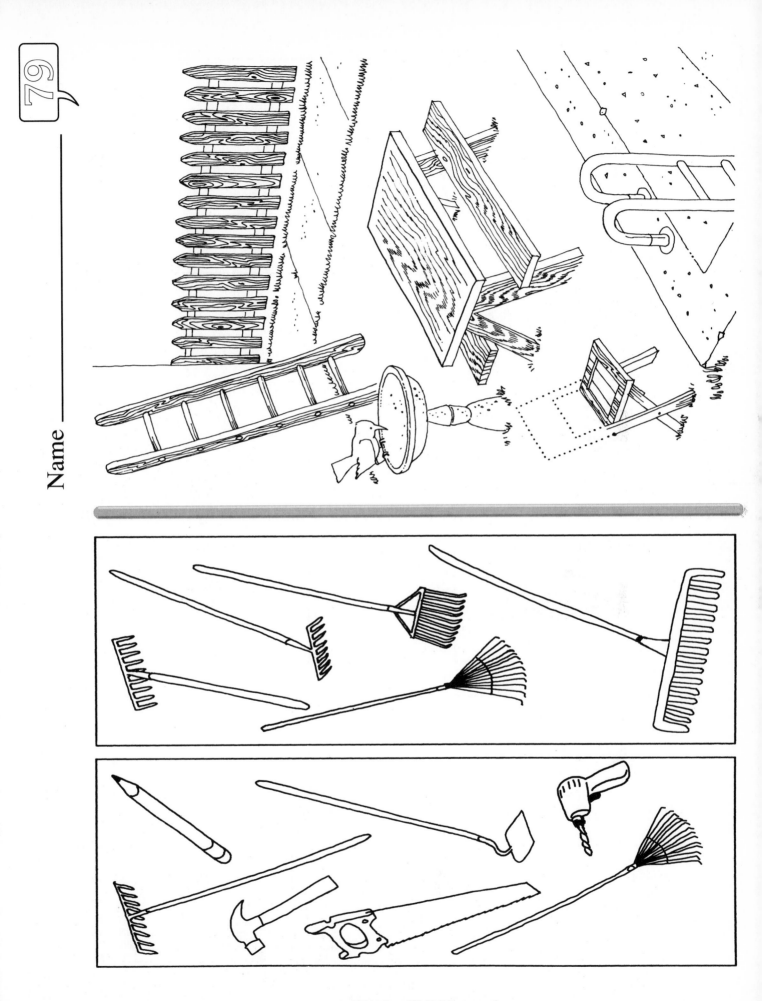

79

Name _____

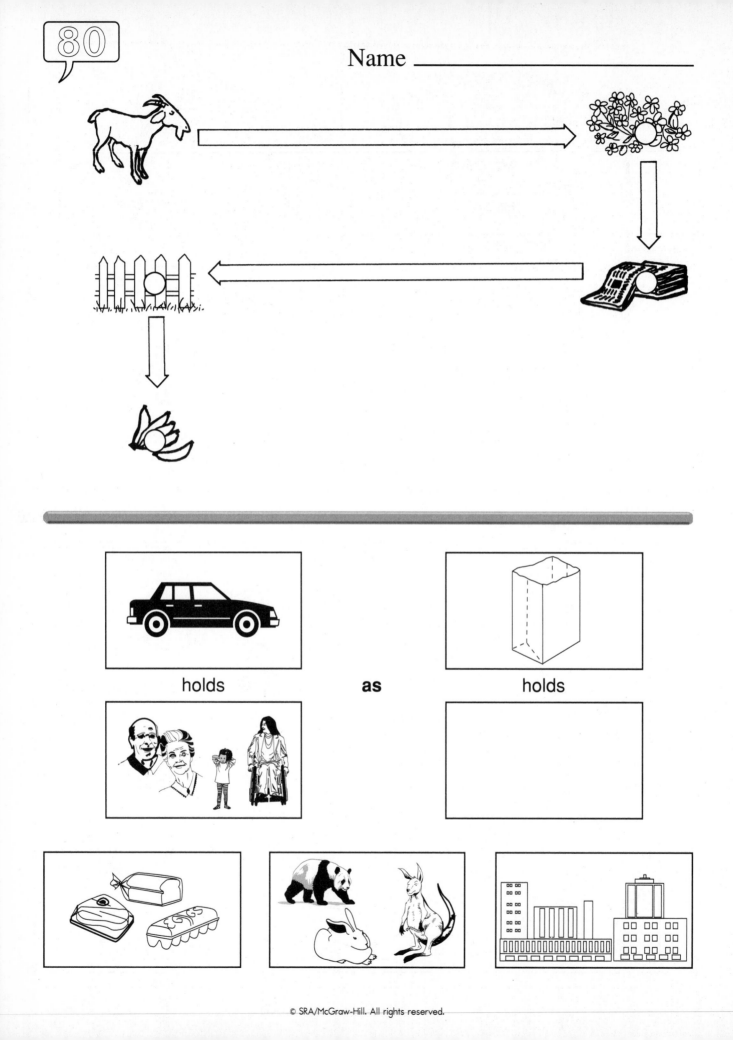

holds   **as**   holds

Name _____

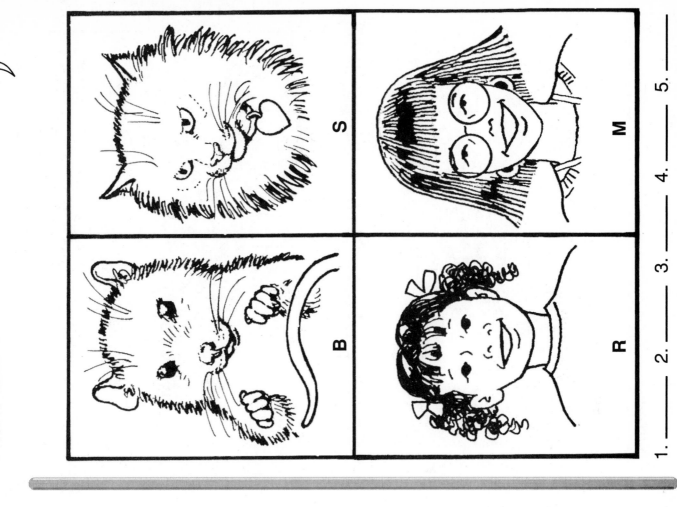

S

M

B

R

1. _____ 2. _____ 3. _____ 4. _____ 5. _____

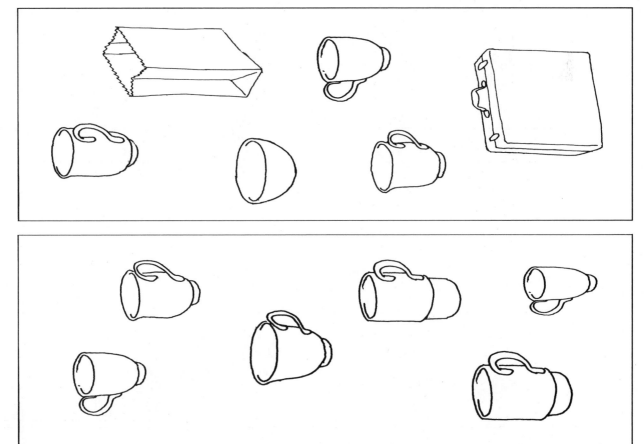

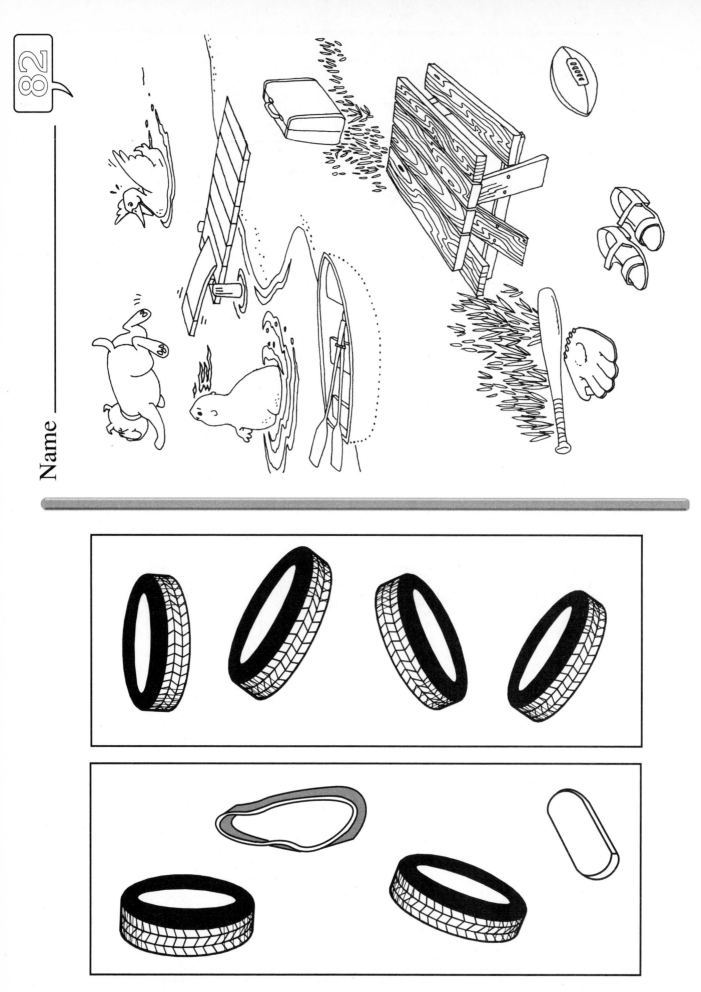

82

Name _____

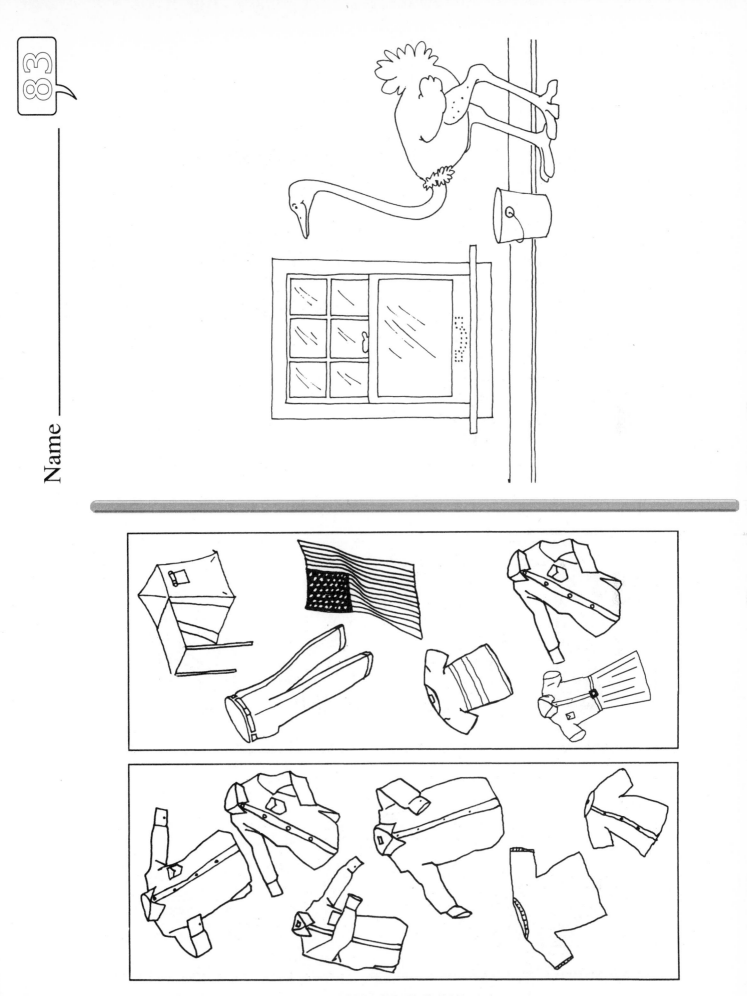

Name

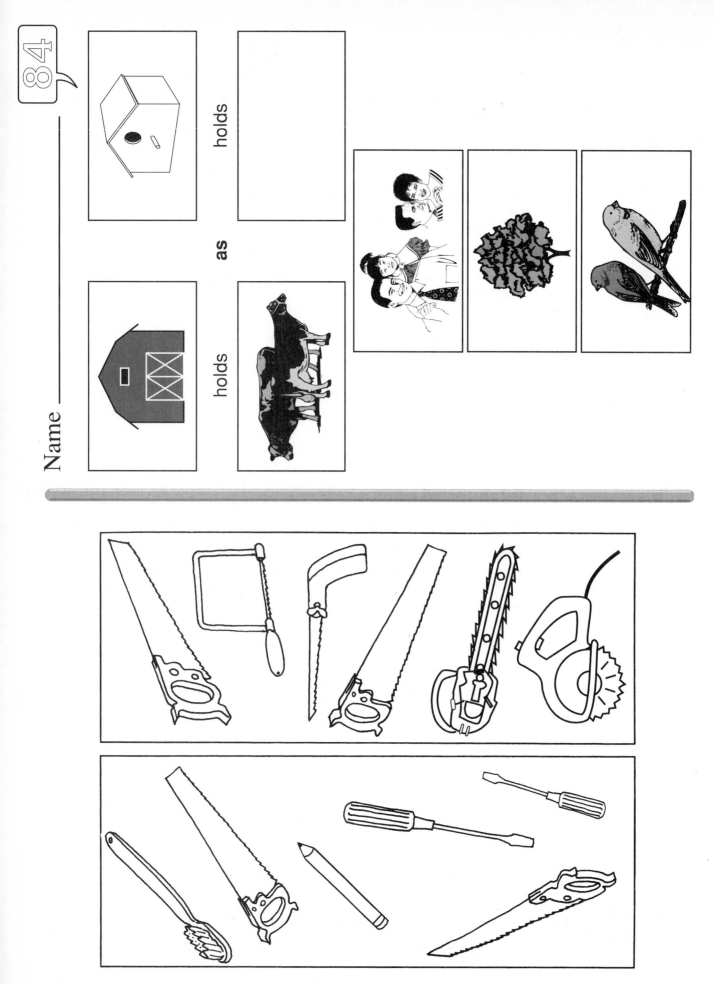

Name _____

84

holds

as

holds

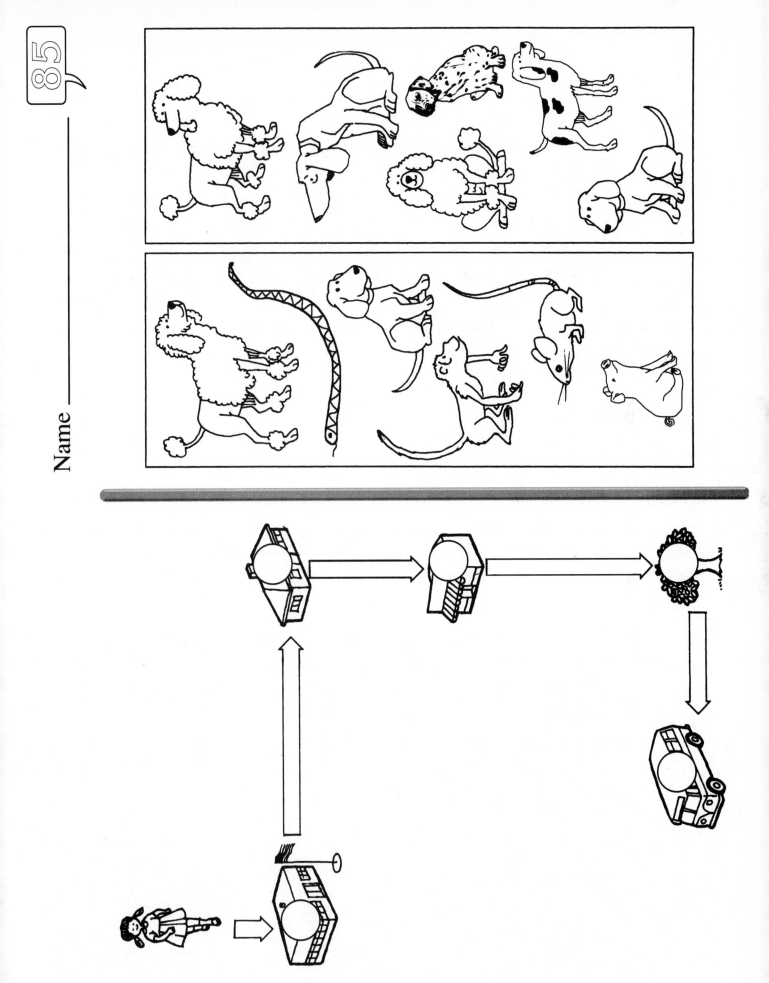

85

Name _____

Name _____

					1. ____
					2. ____
					3. ____
R	P	B	C	S	4. ____
					5. ____
					6. ____

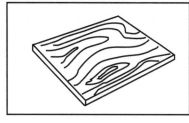

does work with **as** does work with

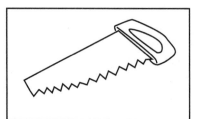

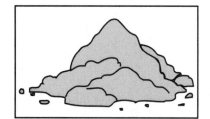

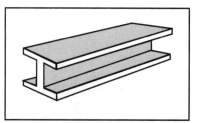

87

Name _____

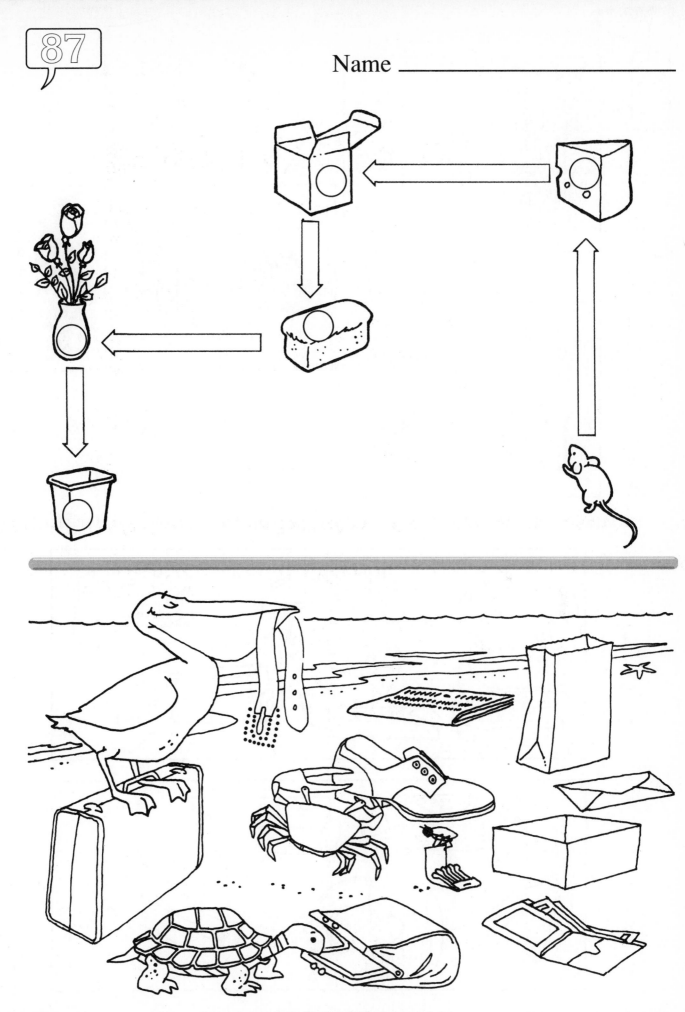

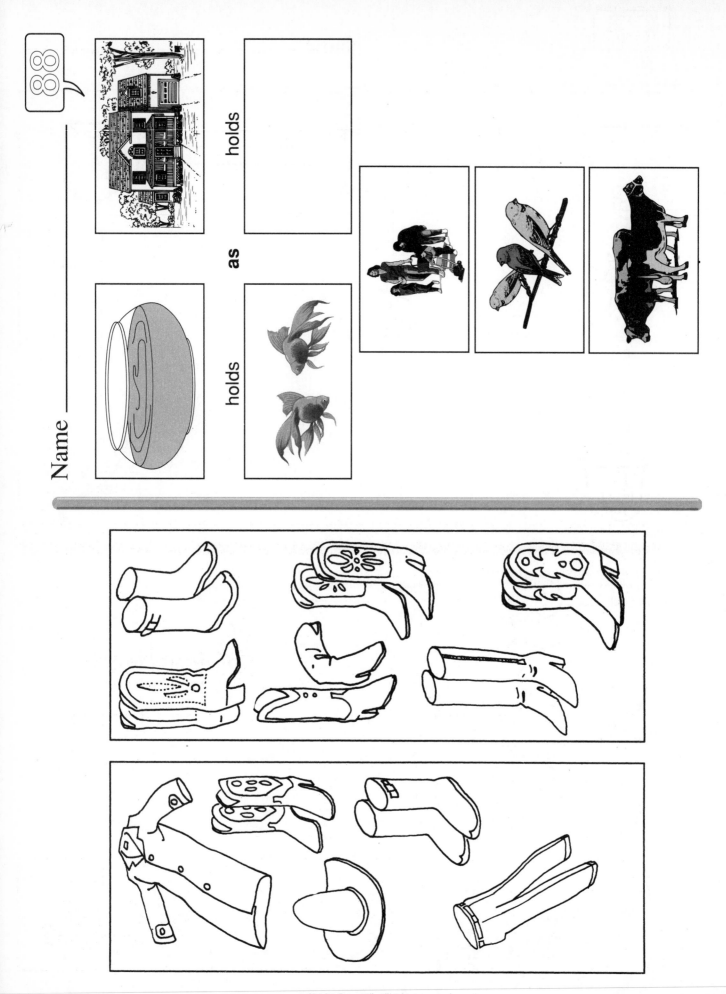

Name _____

88

holds

as

holds

Name _____

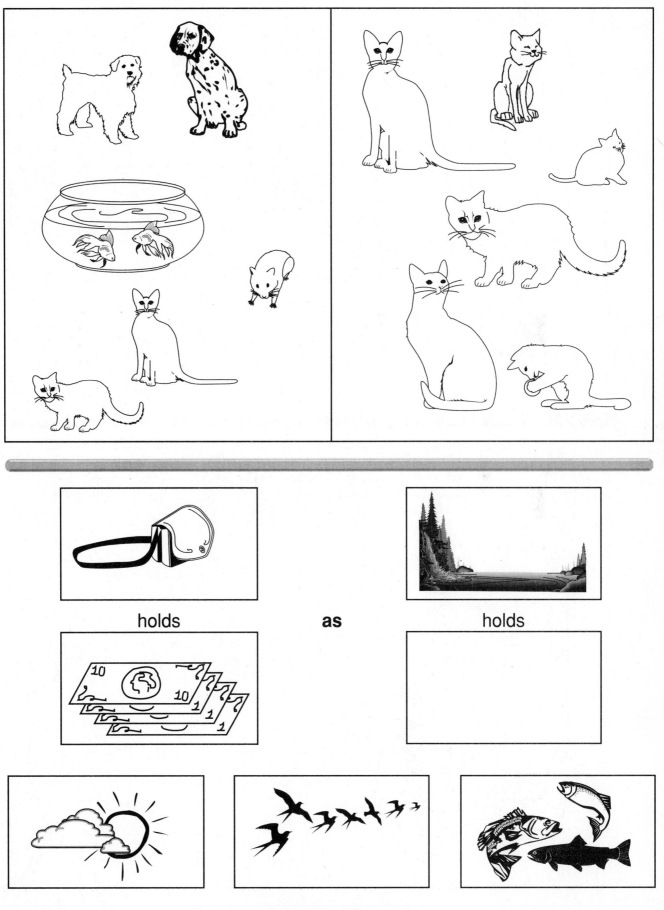

holds   **as**   holds

Name

Name _____

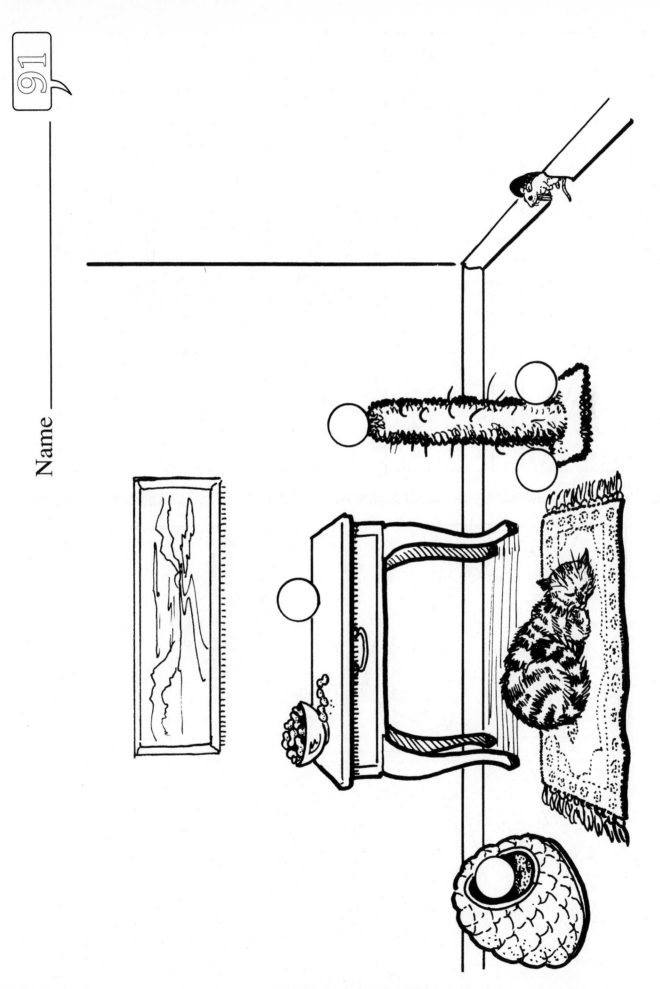

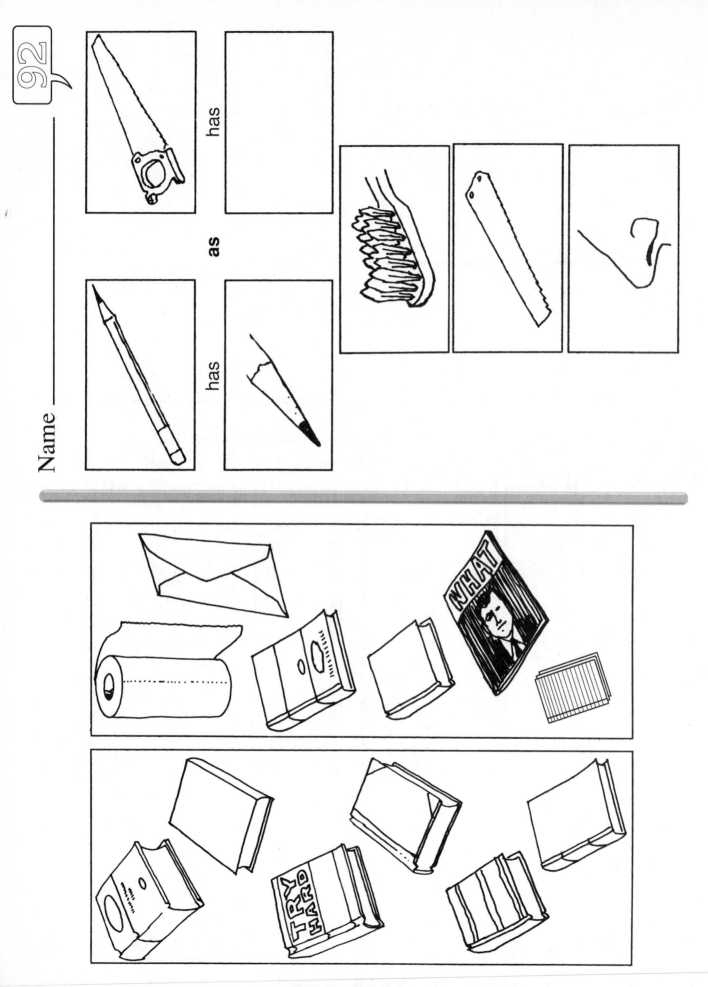

Name

as

has

has

WHAT

TRY HARD

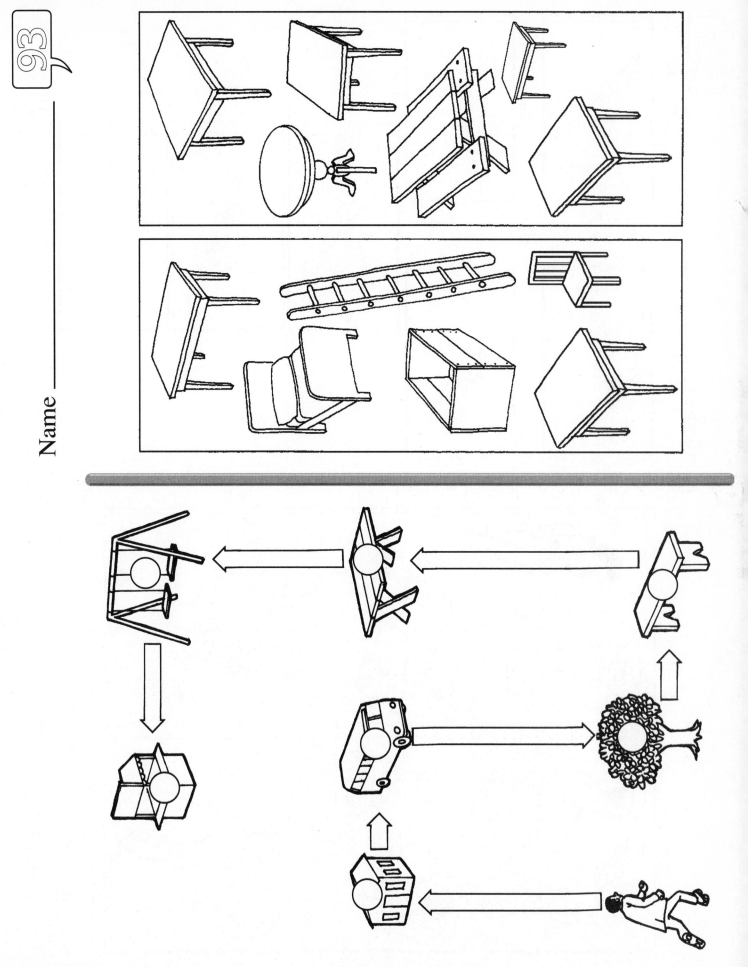

Name

93

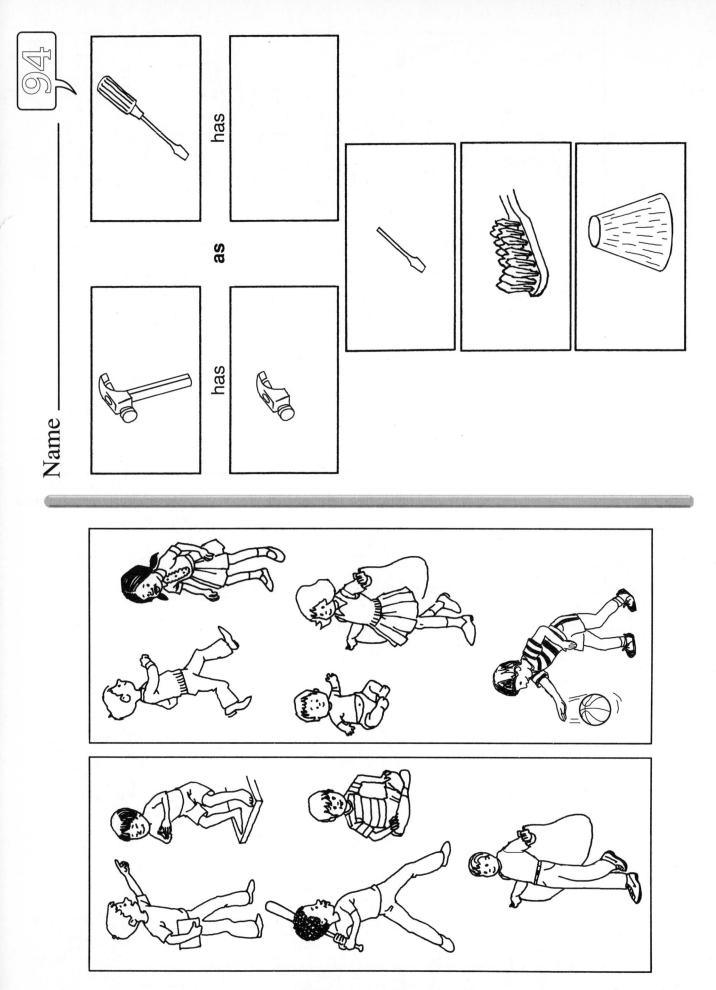

94

Name _____

has

as

has

Name _____

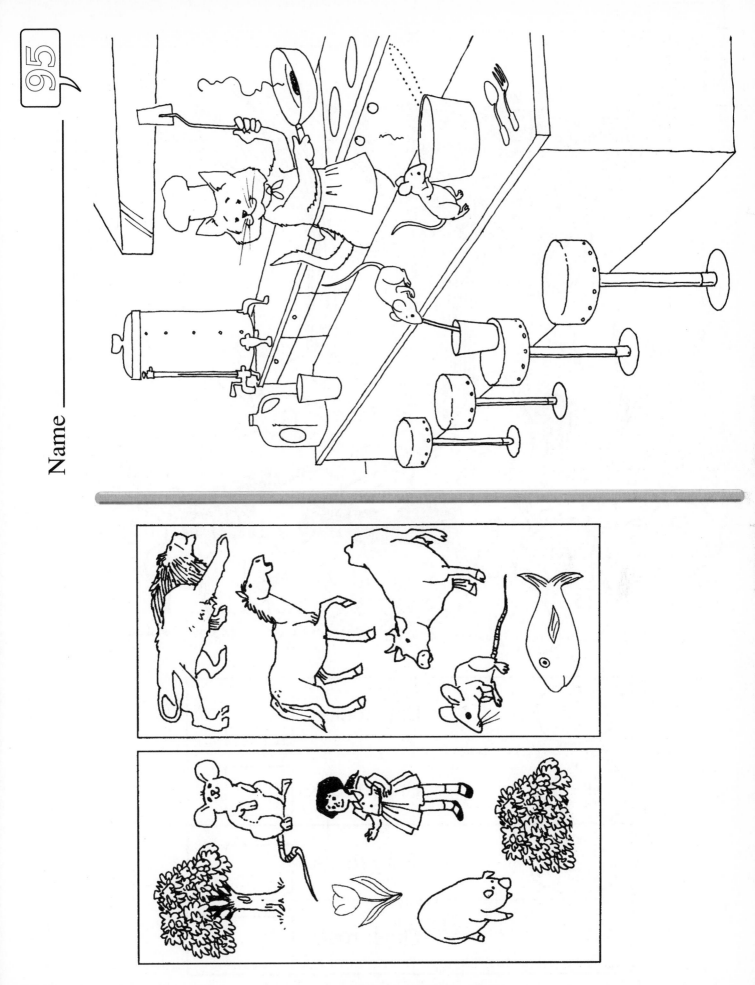

Name _____

P	Pink rocks	
B	Brown rocks	
G	Gray rocks	
	Other rocks	

Name _____

tools   plants

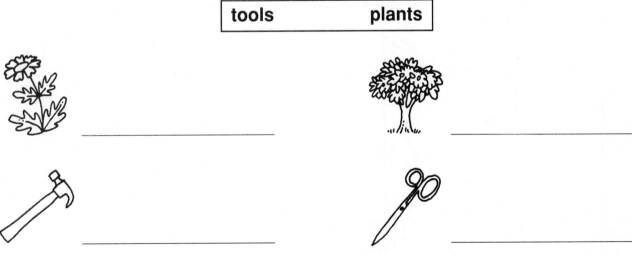

_____   _____

_____   _____

98

Name _____

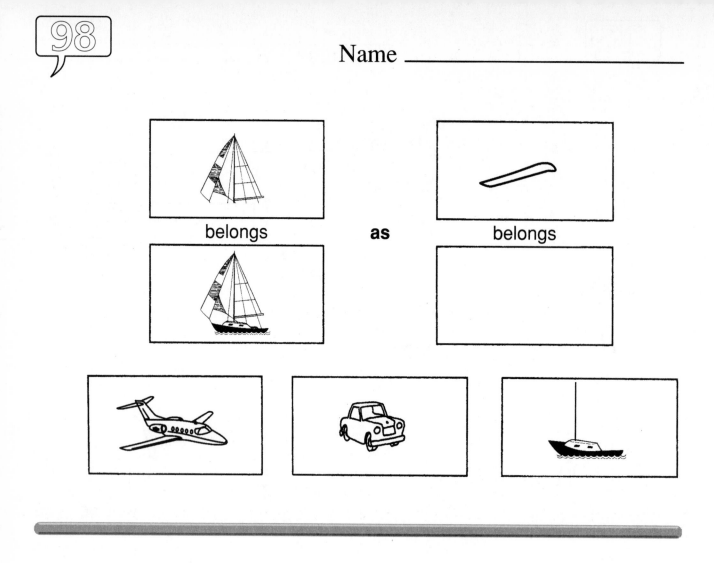

belongs   as   belongs

food   vehicles

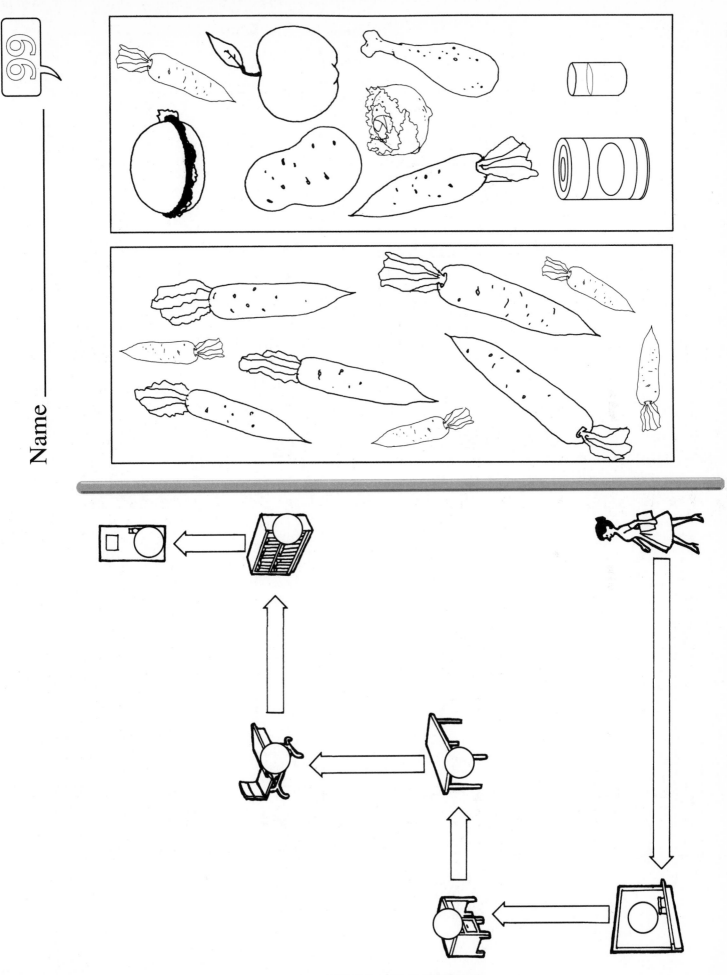

99

Name _____

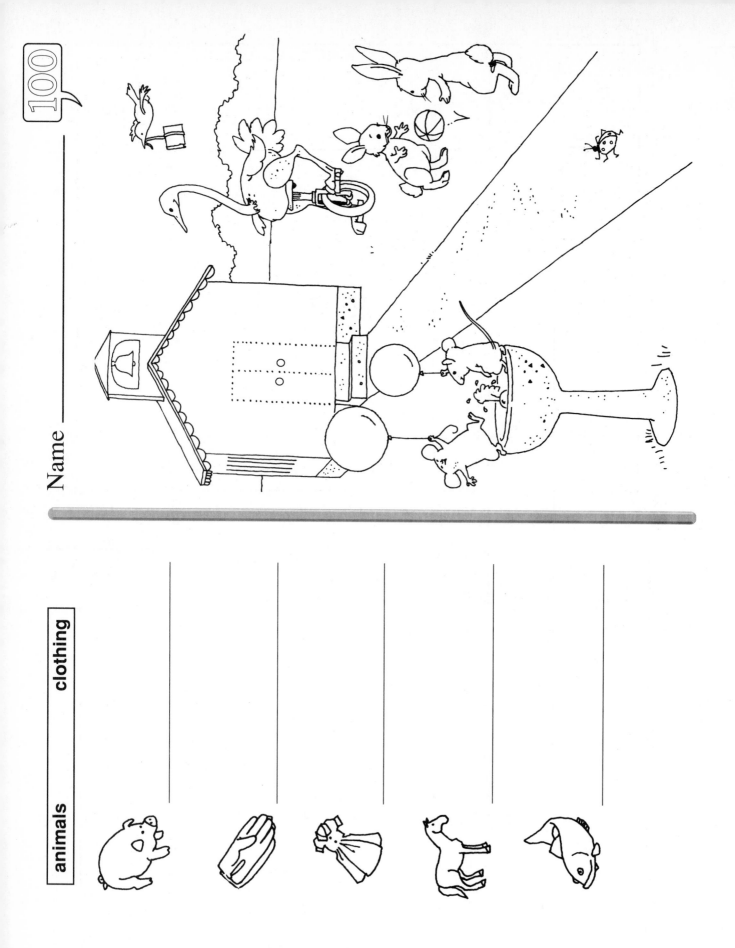

animals   **clothing**

Name _____

R bird	Red birds		
Y bird	Yellow birds		
B bird	Blue birds		
	Other animals		

Name _____

has

as

has

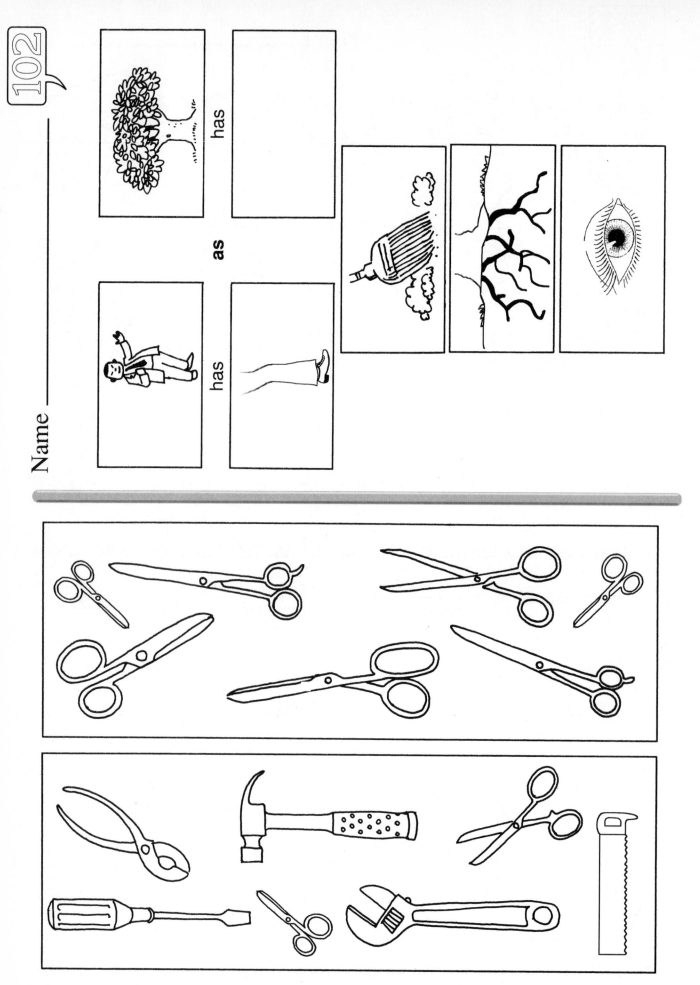

Name _____

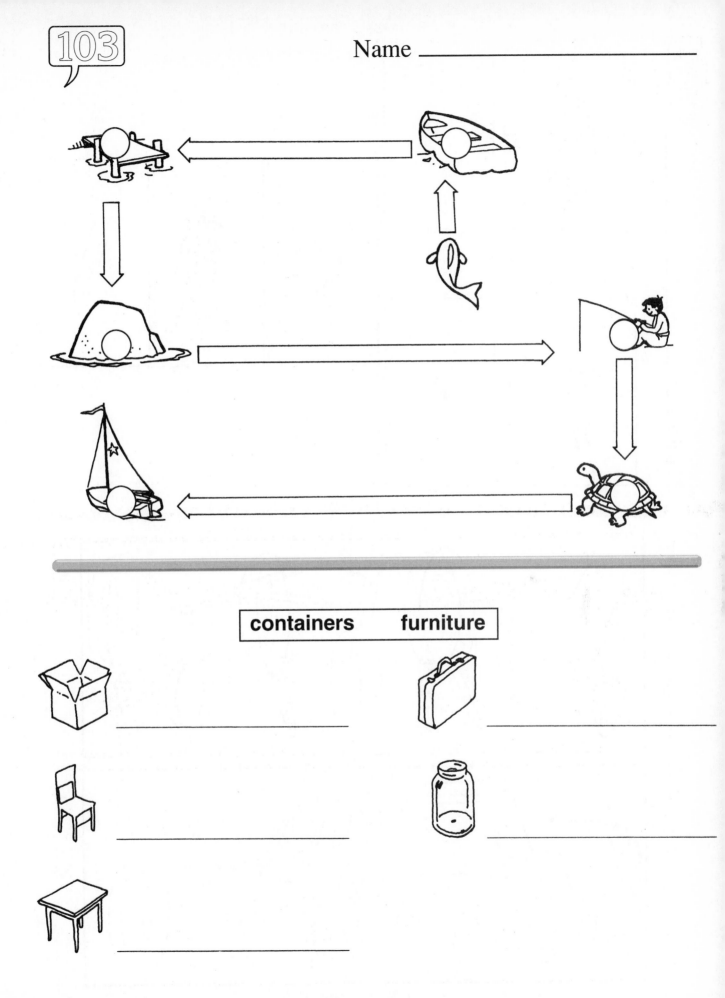

containers	furniture

_____

_____

_____

_____

_____

104

Name _____

has

as

has

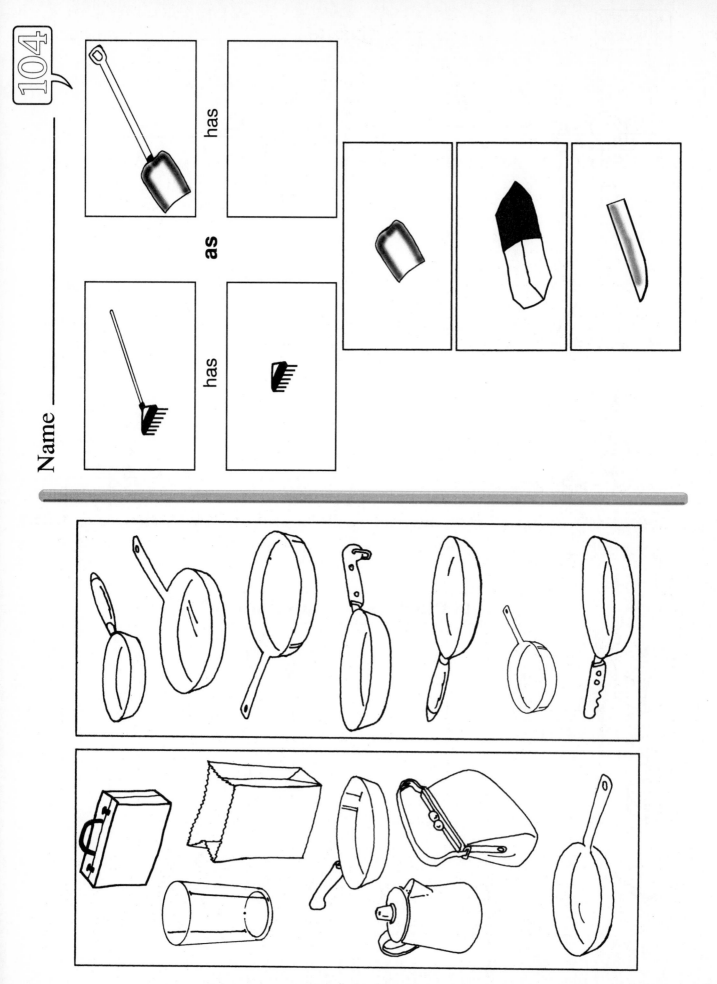

Name _____

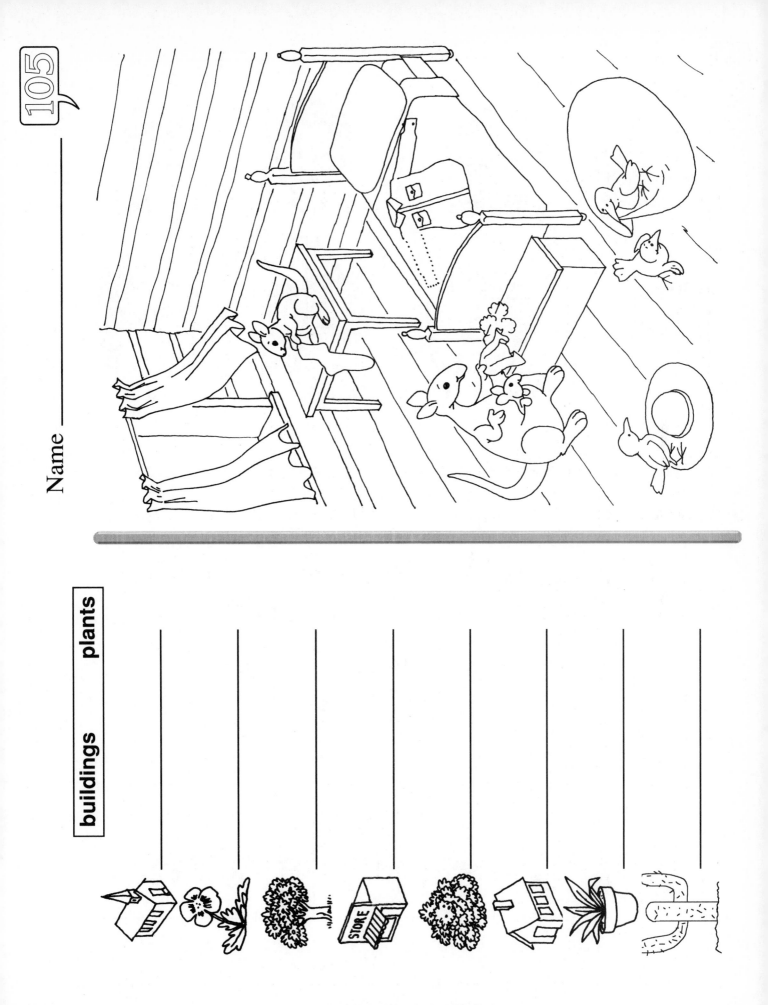

buildings   plants

105

106

Name _____

Sweetie

Bleep

Roger

Paul

Roxie

Bragging Rat

Clarabelle

Rolla

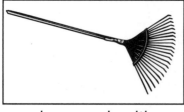

does work with **as** does work with

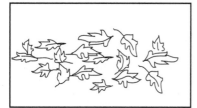

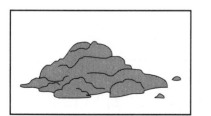

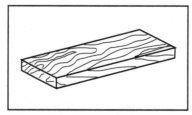

107

Name _____

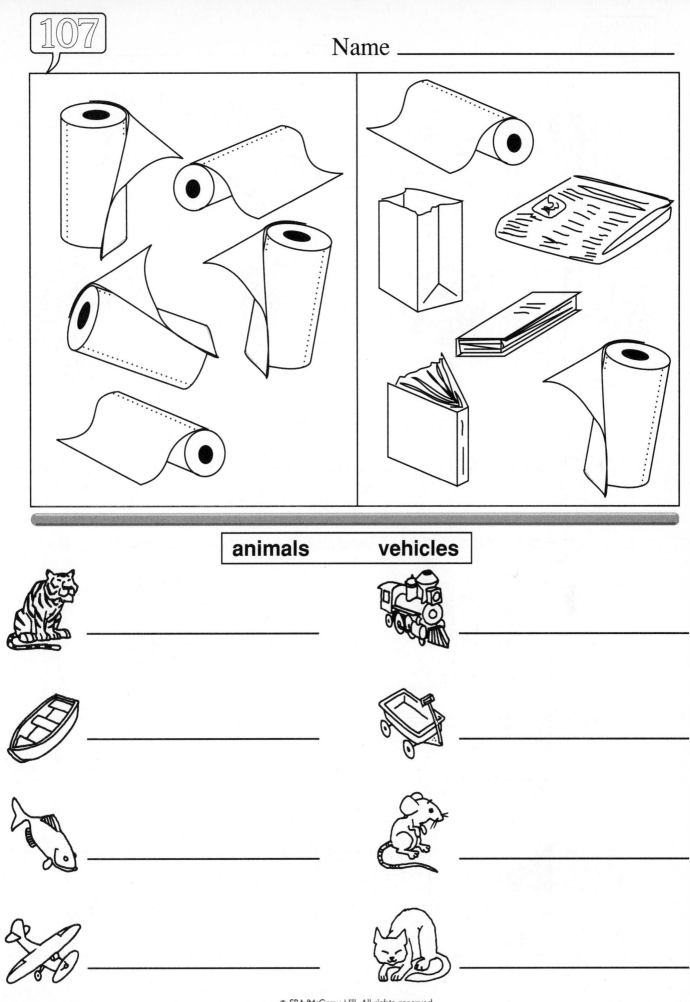

animals   vehicles

Name _____

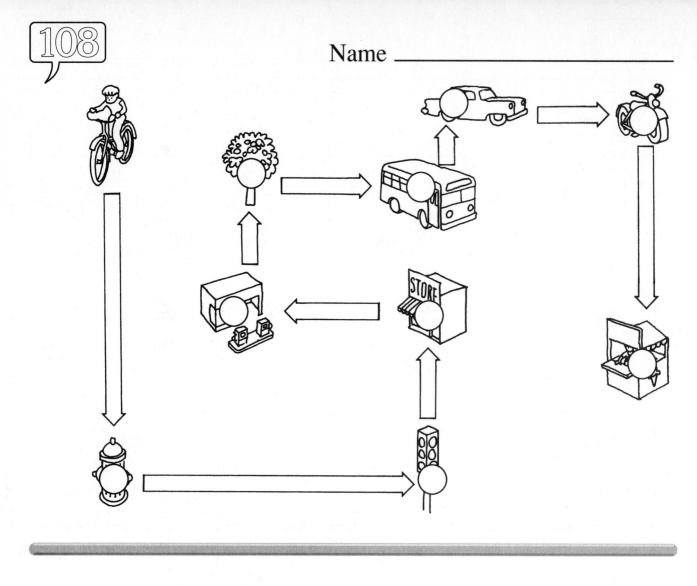

has · **as** · has

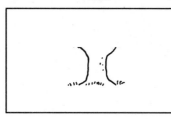 

 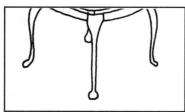 

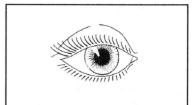

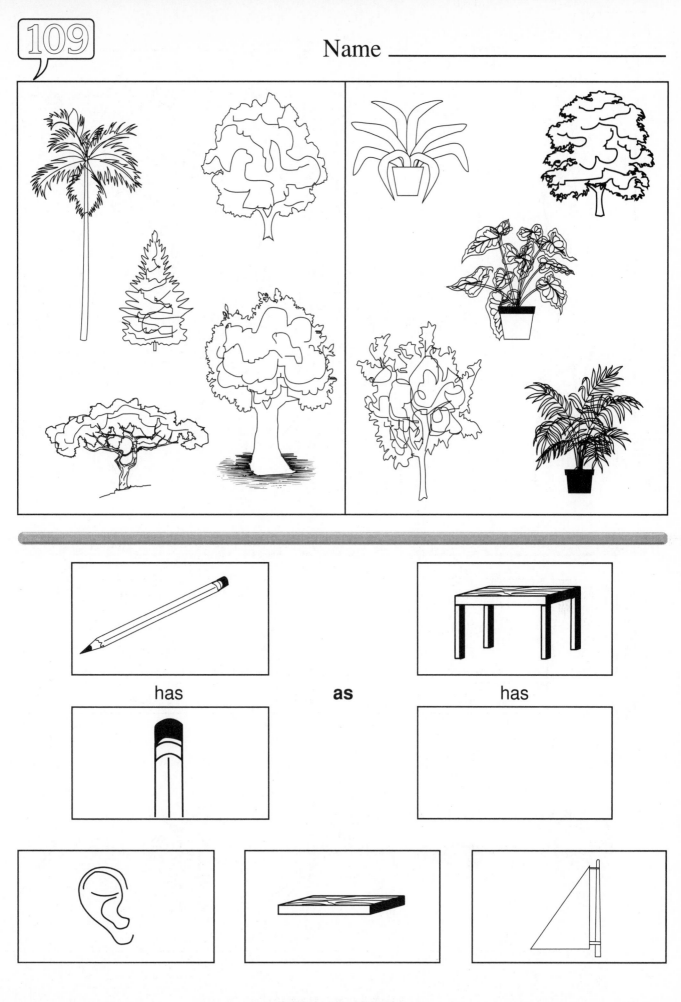

has

as

has

Name _____

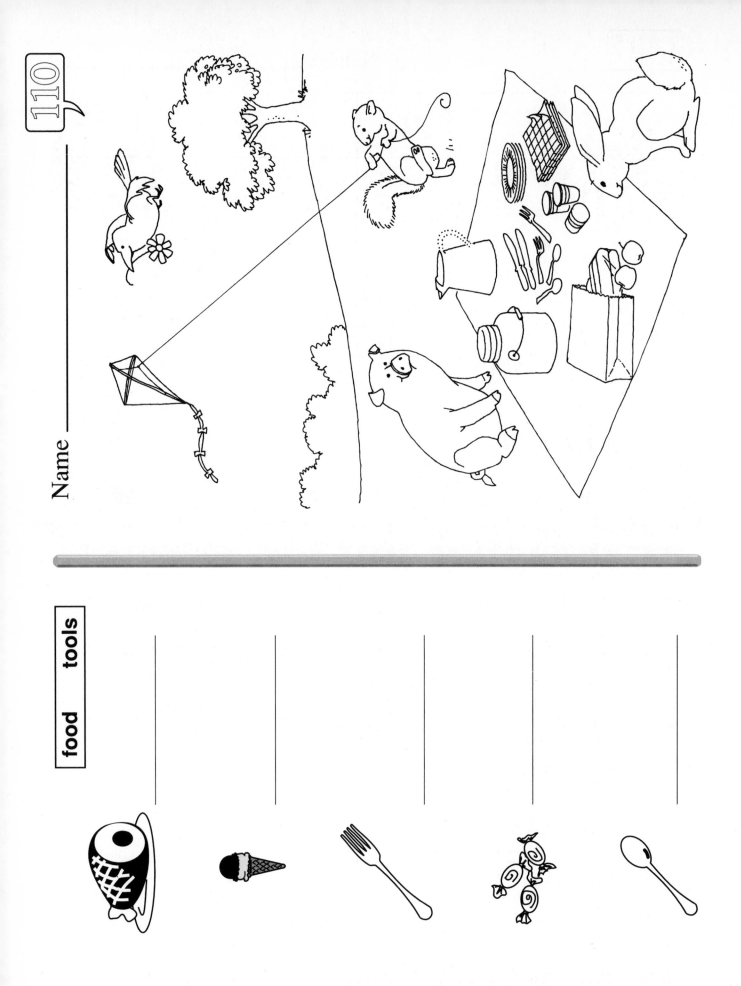

food	tools

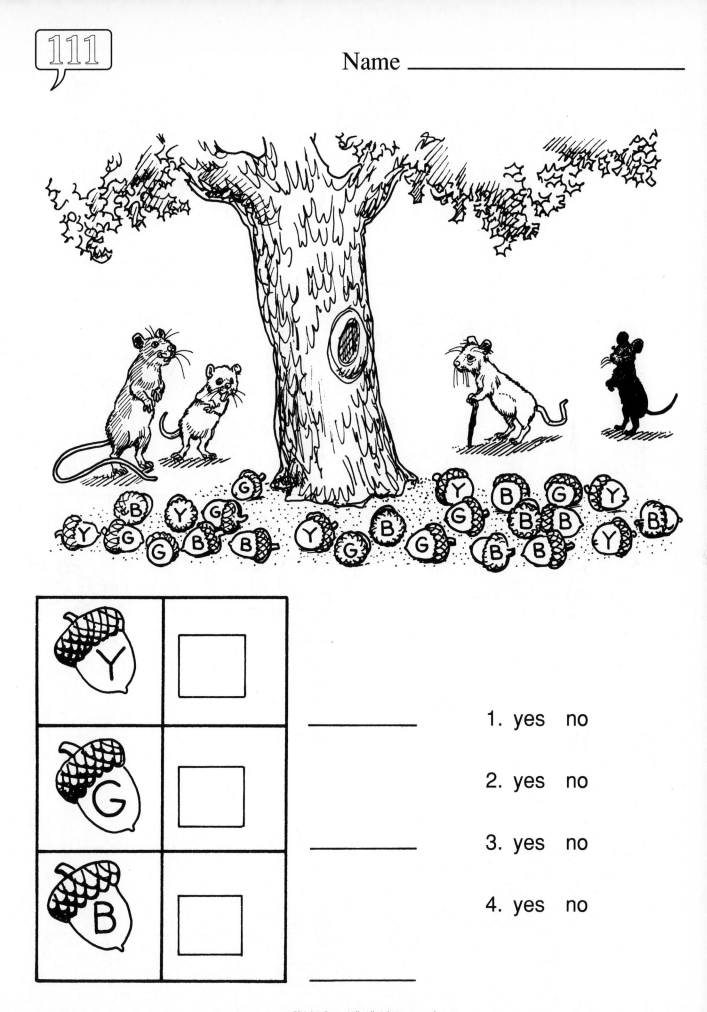

111

Name _____

1. yes no

2. yes no

3. yes no

4. yes no

Name

113

Name _____

furniture	plants

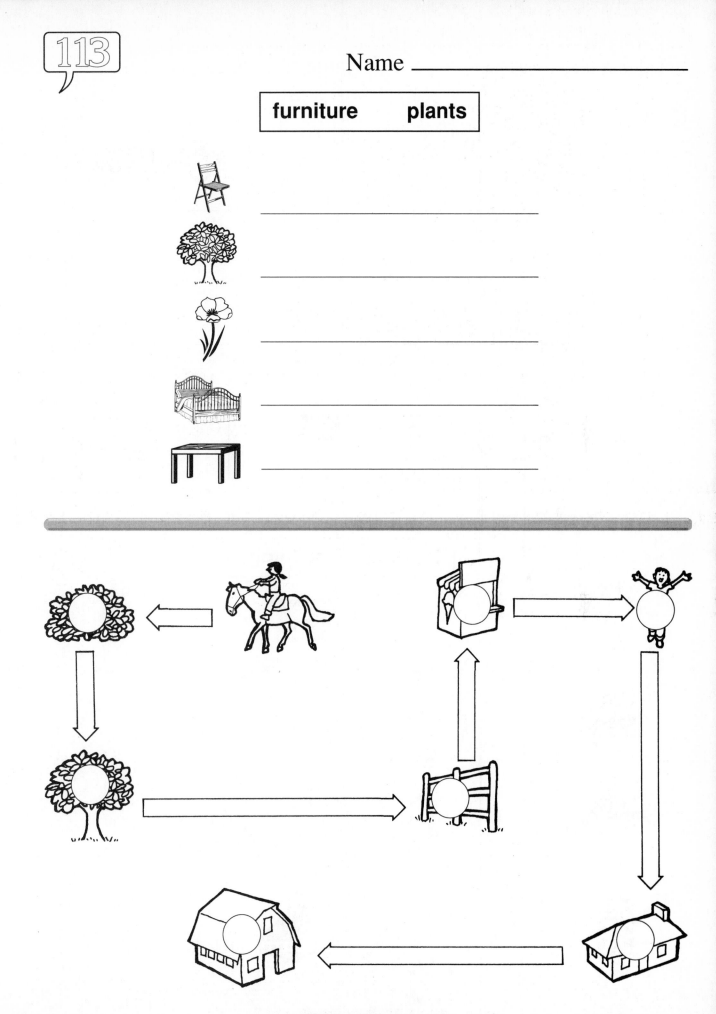

Name _____

has   **as**   has

clothing   buildings

_____   _____

_____   _____

_____   _____

_____   _____

Name _____

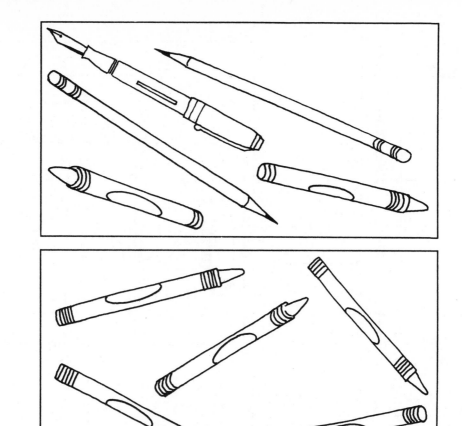

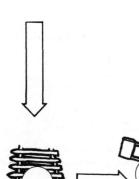

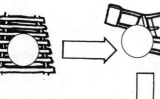

Name _____

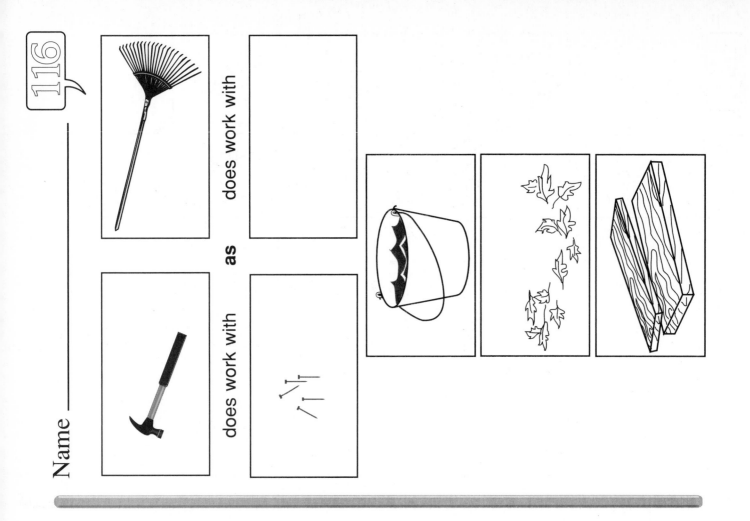

rake does work with _____ as hammer does work with _____

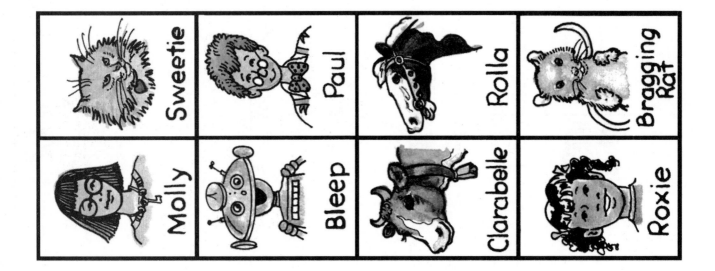

Sweetie

Paul

Rolla

Bragging Rat

Molly

Bleep

Clarabelle

Roxie

Name _____

117

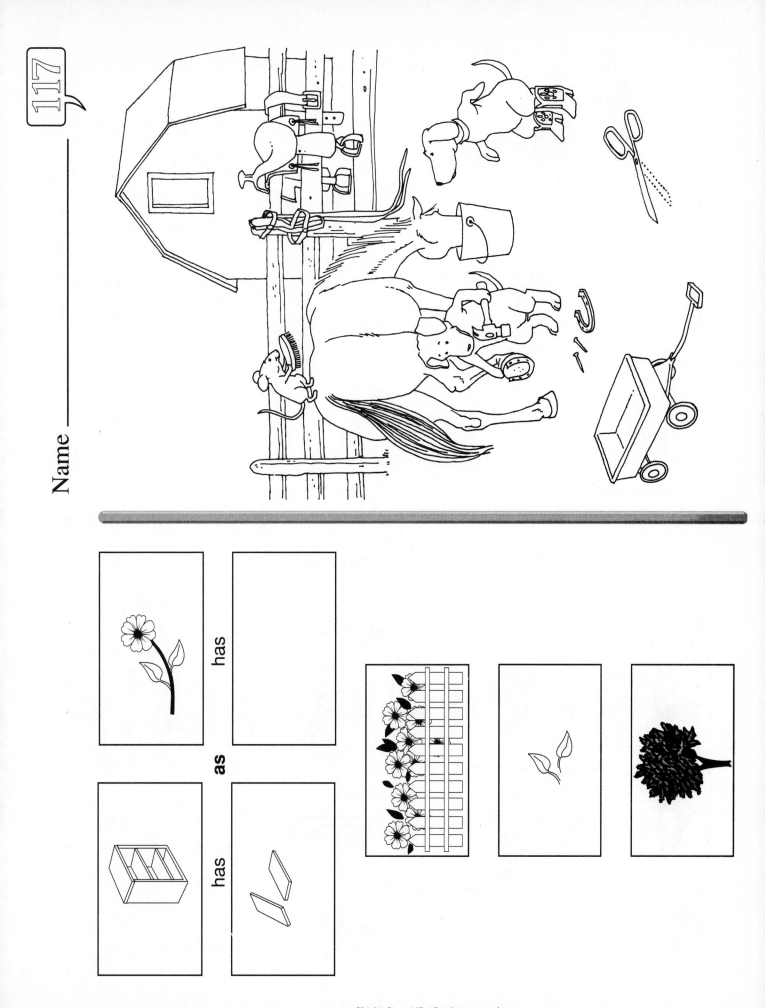

has

as

has

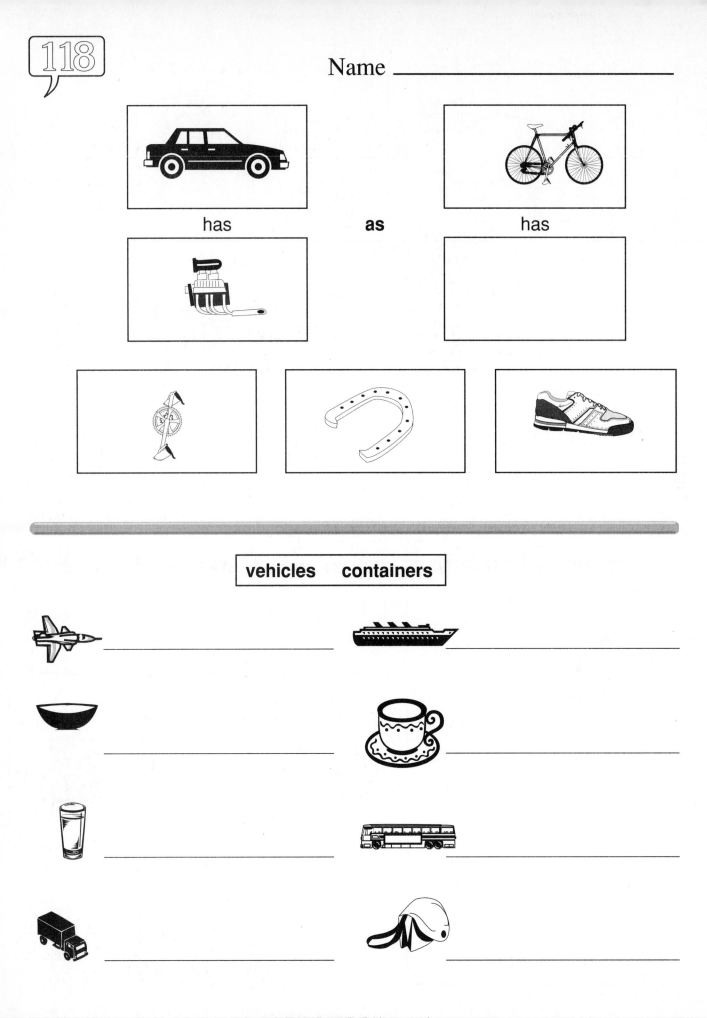

118

has   **as**   has

vehicles   containers

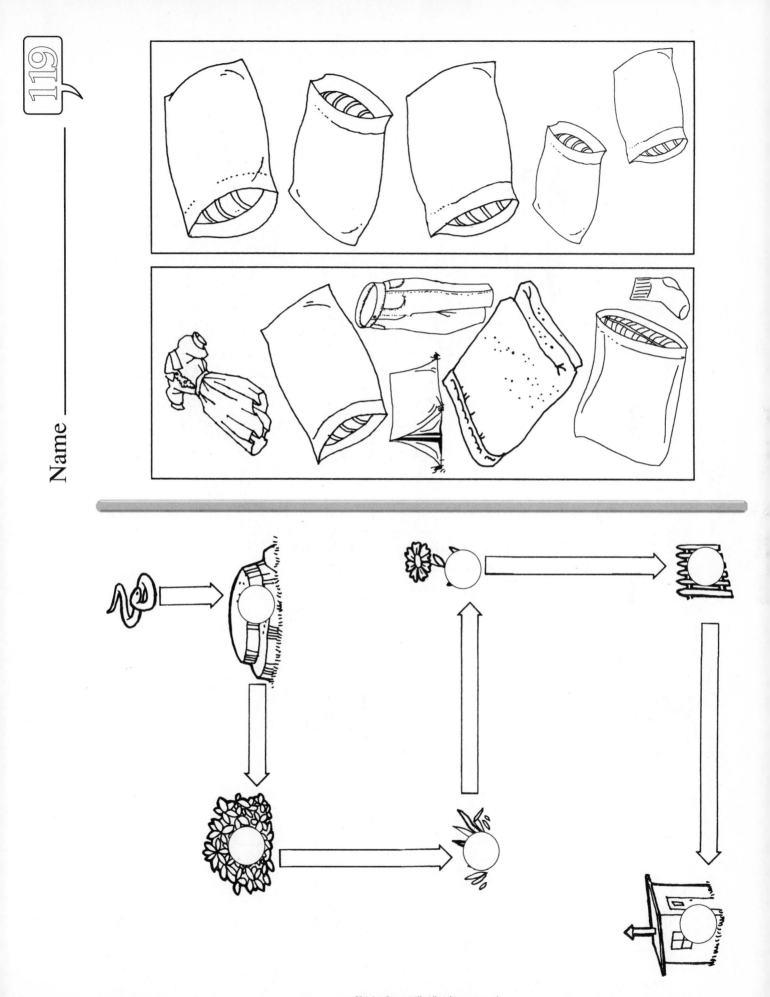

Name _____

containers	animals

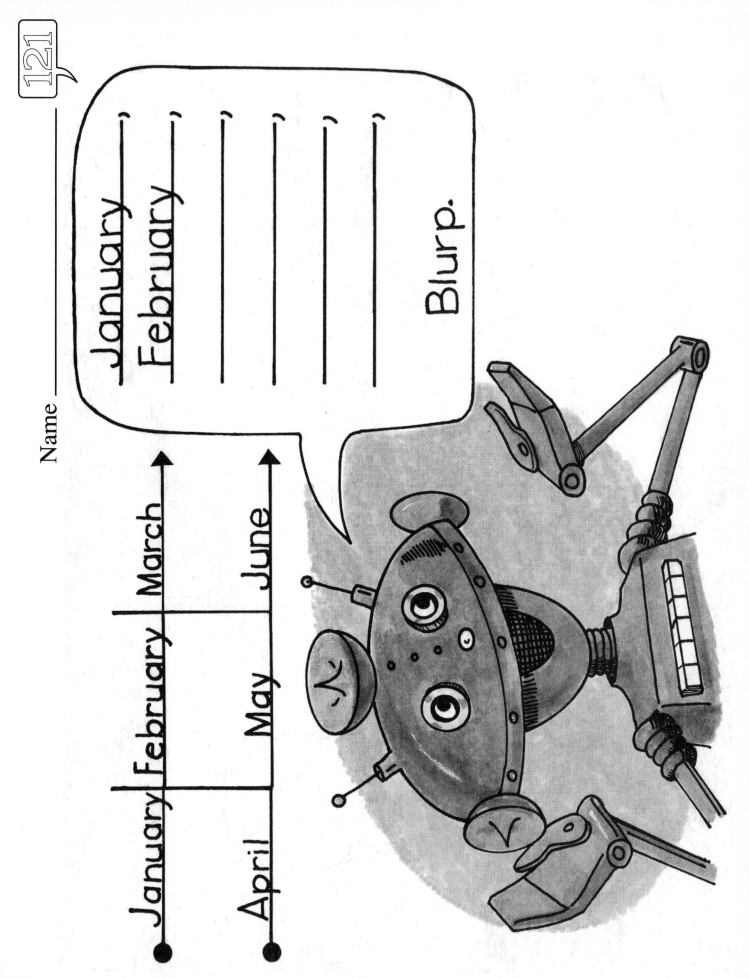

Name

January
February
_____
_____
_____
_____

Blurp.

January February March

April May June

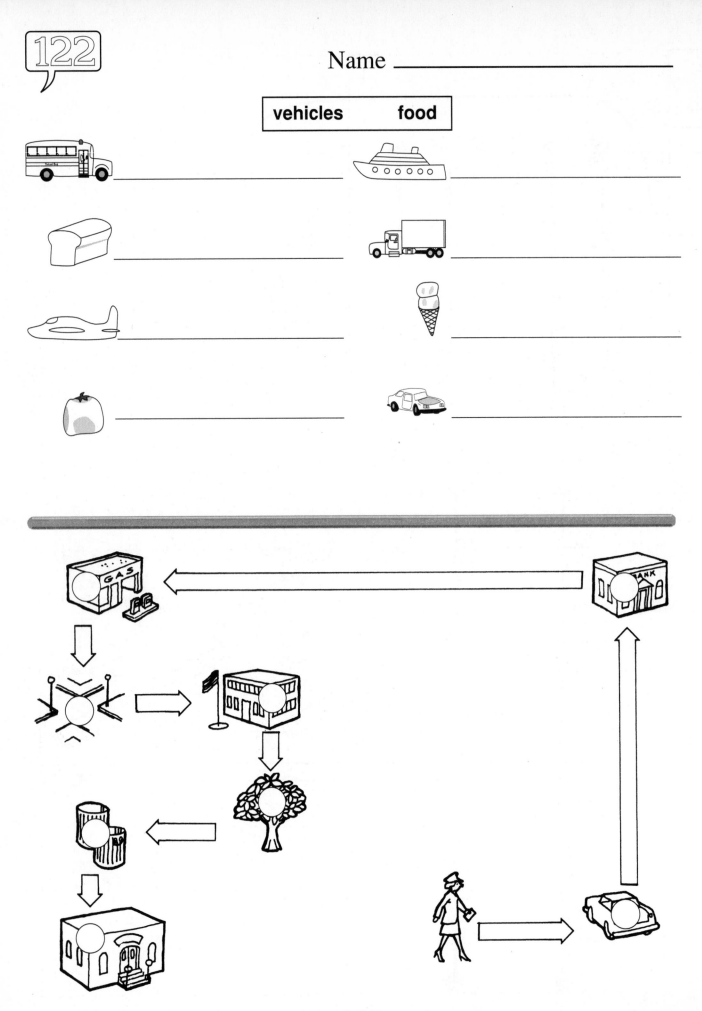

Name _____

has

as

has

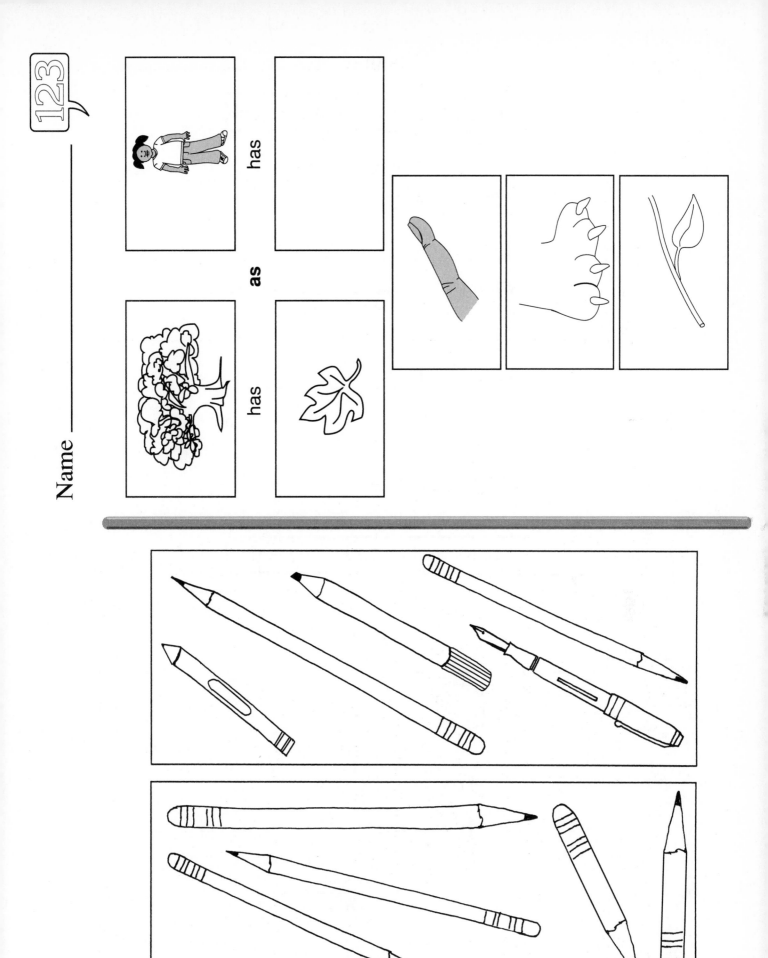

Name _____

| rough | tall | old | pull |

1. push _____

2. young _____

3. smooth _____

4. short _____

| tools | furniture | plants |

_____   _____

_____   _____

_____   _____

_____   _____

_____   _____

Name _____

win	dry	short	fast

1. slow _____

2. lose _____

3. wet _____

4. tall _____

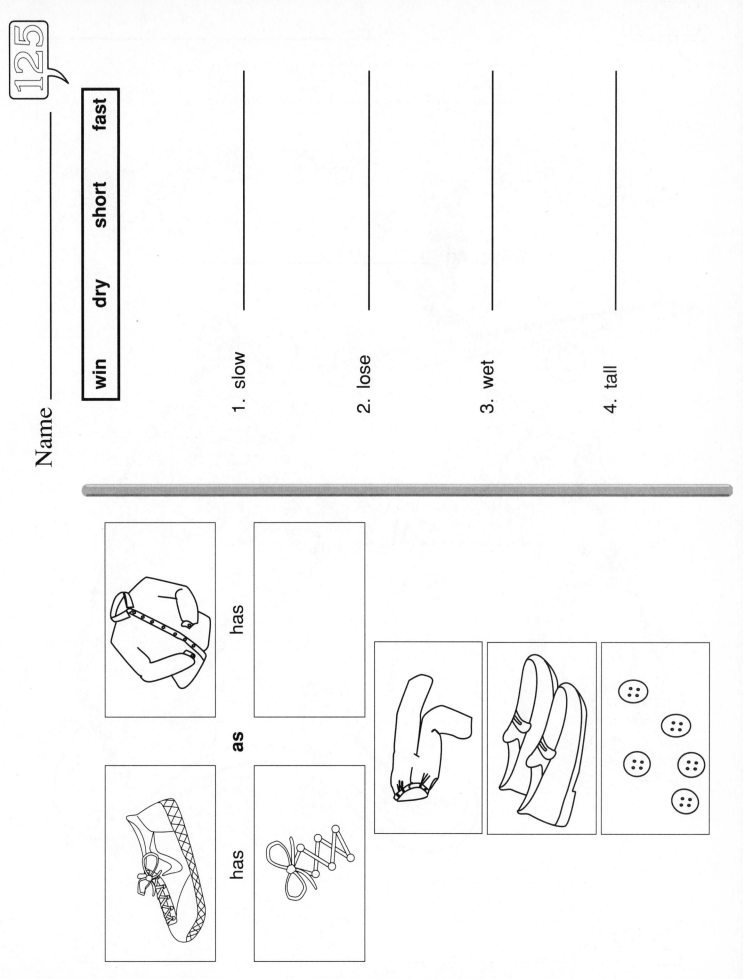

has

as

has

125

Name _____

127

Name _____

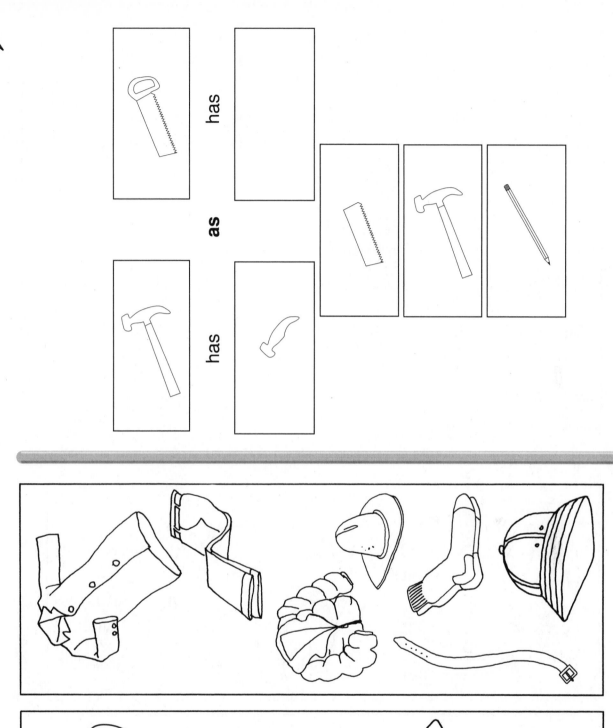

has ___ as ___ has

Name _____

big	win	push	smooth	open

1. rough _____

2. lose _____

3. shut _____

4. pull _____

5. small _____

129

Name _____

vehicles	colors	plants

truck _____

tree _____

ship _____

green _____

van _____

weed _____

pink _____

yellow _____

grass _____

red _____

Name _____

| deep | easy | raw | clean | near |

1. cooked _____

2. shallow _____

3. far _____

4. dirty _____

5. hard _____

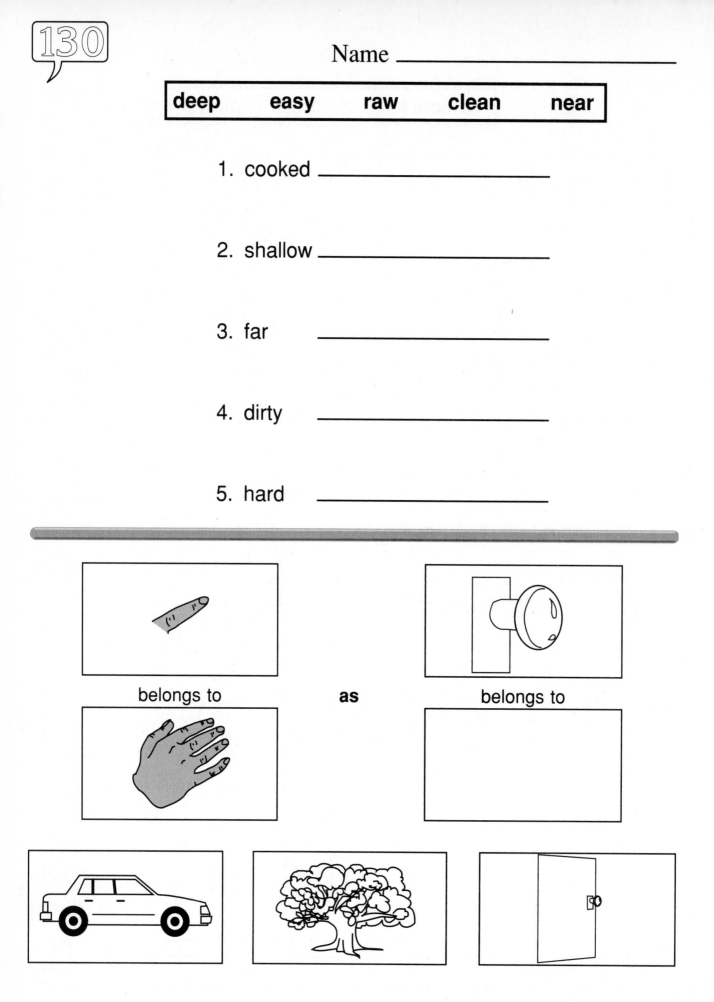

belongs to **as** belongs to

Name _____

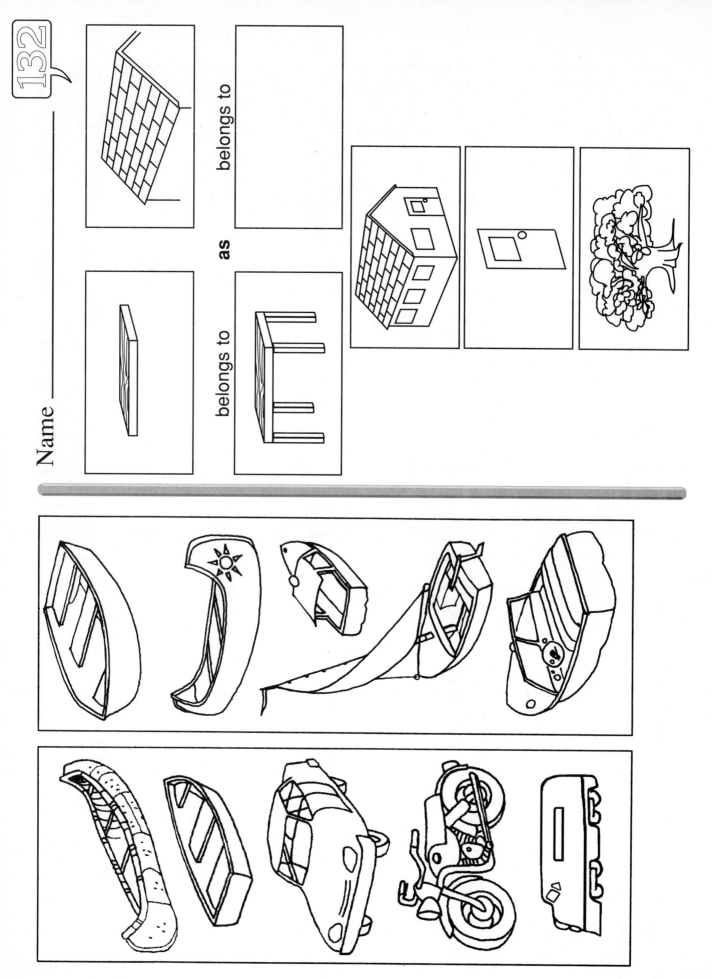

belongs to

as

belongs to

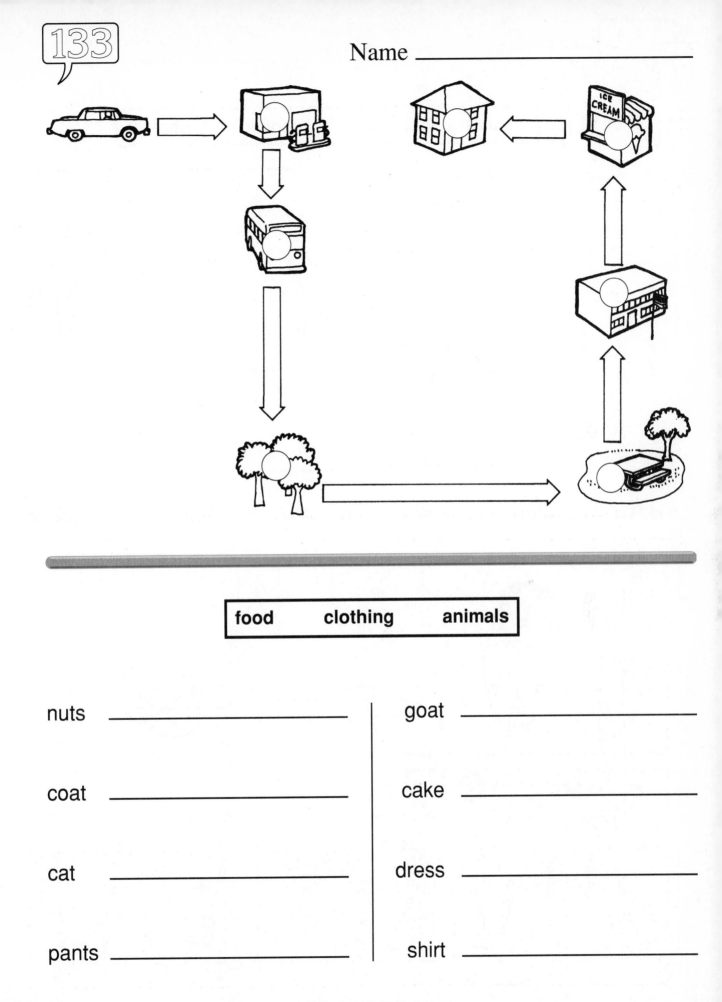

133

Name _____

food   clothing   animals

nuts _____   goat _____

coat _____   cake _____

cat _____   dress _____

pants _____   shirt _____

Name _____

quiet	shallow	cooked	short

1. long _____

2. deep _____

3. loud _____

4. raw _____

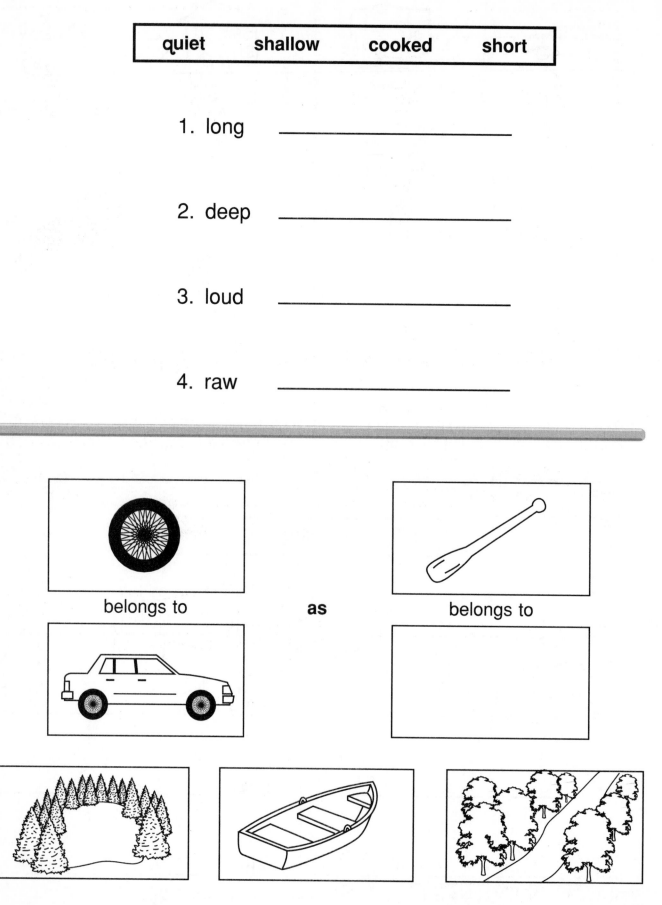

belongs to   as   belongs to

Name _____

Name _____

1. bud   2. yus   3. fud   4. ugg

_____ _____ _____ _____

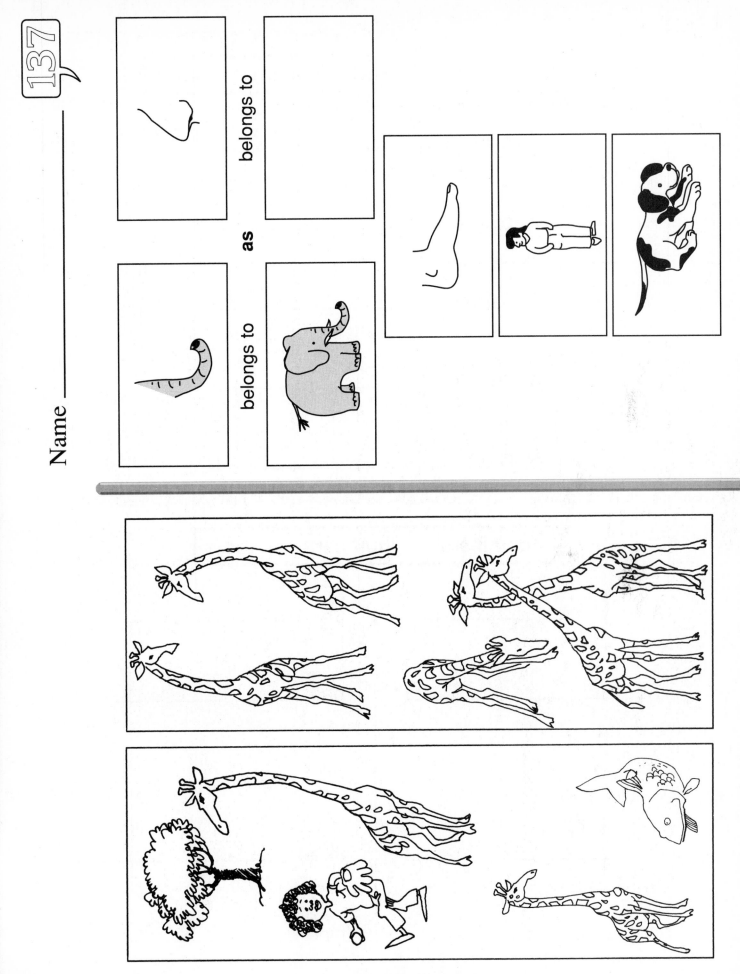

Name _____

137

belongs to   as   belongs to

Name _____

wide	shiny	pull	short	long

1. tall _____

2. push _____

3. narrow _____

4. dull _____

5. short _____

containers	numbers	tools

jar _____   six _____

saw _____   bag _____

ten _____   rake _____

cup _____   three _____

mop _____   nine _____

Name _____

| cry | short | difficult | wide | dark |

1. easy _____

2. laugh _____

3. light _____

4. narrow _____

5. tall _____

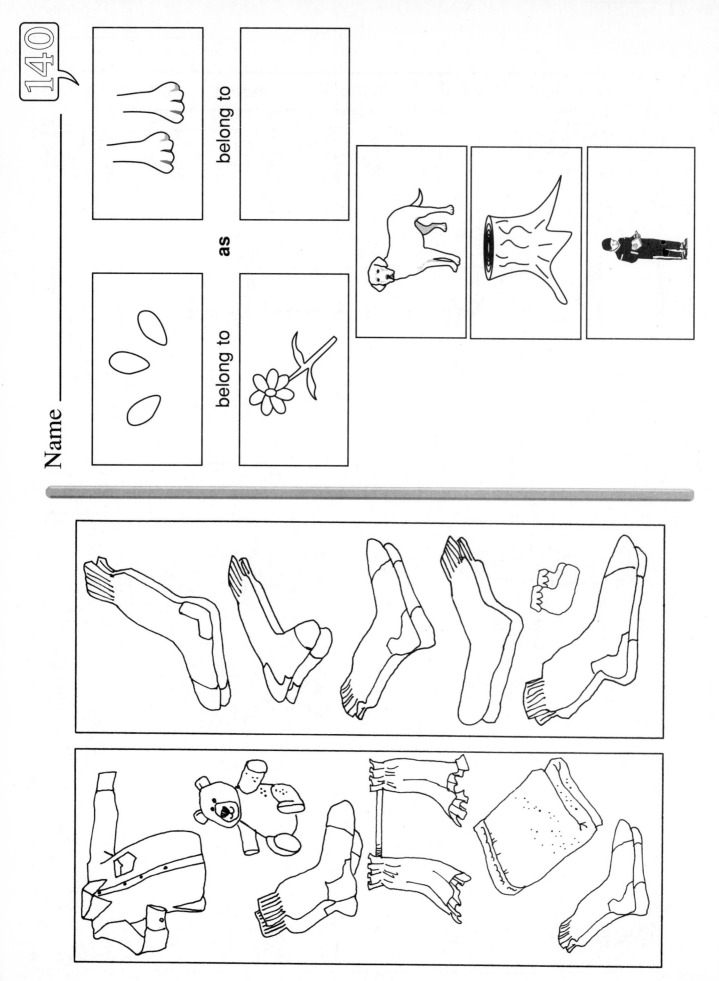

Name

140

belong to

as

belong to

Name _____

Name _____

sad	clean	push	near	dirty

1. dirty   _____

2. clean   _____

3. far   _____

4. happy   _____

5. pull   _____

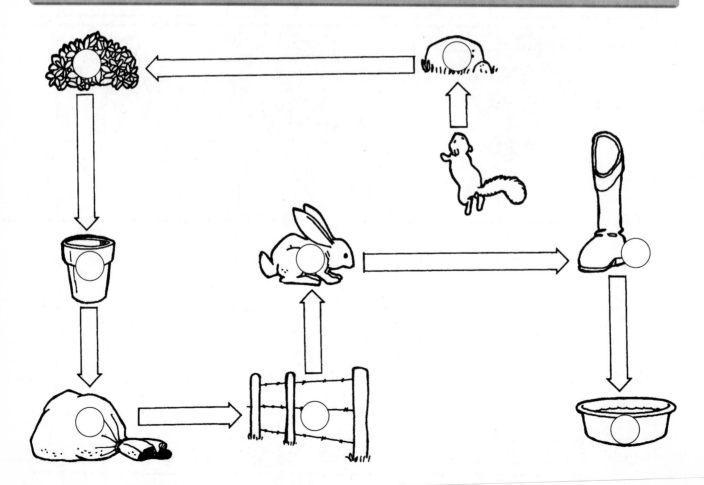

143

Name _____

belong to **as** belong to

| vehicles | animals | clothing |

sock _____   turtle _____

boat _____   tractor _____

shark _____   mole _____

hat _____   dress _____

train _____   car _____

Name _____

open	happy	big	weak	shiny

1. small _____

2. shut _____

3. dull _____

4. strong _____

5. sad _____

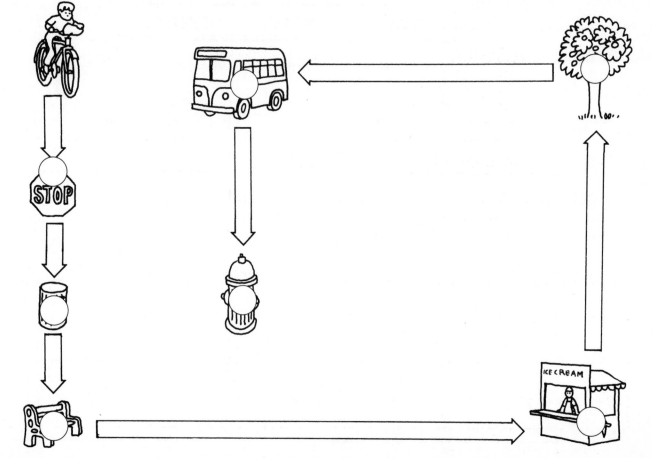

Name _____

dirty	slow	raw	dark	skinny

1. cooked _____

2. light _____

3. fat _____

4. clean _____

5. fast _____

is made of   **as**   is made of